BIBLE KEY WORDS

X. FAITH

In the same series

LOVE

THE CHURCH

SIN

RIGHTEOUSNESS

GNOSIS

APOSTLESHIP

BASILEIA

LORD

SPIRIT OF GOD

In preparation

LAW

WRATH

LIFE

DEATH

HOPE

BIBLE KEY WORDS
FROM GERHARD KITTEL'S
*THEOLOGISCHES WÖRTERBUCH
ZUM NEUEN TESTAMENT*

FAITH

BY
RUDOLF BULTMANN
and ARTUR WEISER

ADAM & CHARLES BLACK
LONDON

FIRST PUBLISHED 1961
A. AND C. BLACK LIMITED
4, 5 AND 6 SOHO SQUARE, LONDON W.1

Translation from the German
by Dorothea M. Barton, M.A.
edited by P. R. Ackroyd, Ph.D.

PRINTED IN GREAT BRITAIN BY
ROBERT CUNNINGHAM AND SONS LTD, ALVA

EDITOR'S PREFACE

This book is a translation of the article *Πίστις*, written by Professors Rudolf Bultmann and Artur Weiser in the *Theologisches Wörterbuch zum Neuen Testament* (TWNT), begun by G. Kittel and now edited by G. Friedrich, Vol. VI, pp. 174-230. Apart from some abbreviations in Chapters II and III, and some curtailing of footnotes, the whole text is here translated. The order of the material differs by the placing of the Old Testament chapter first; cross-reference to the German text may readily be made since the chapter subdivisions coincide.

The 'Word Books' in this series which have already appeared (and others are to follow) make available to the English reader some part of the immense assemblage of material in TWNT, material of great interest to any student of the Old and New Testaments. But a word of caution may not be out of place. Some years ago, a New Testament scholar was heard to remark that the articles in TWNT were being regarded in some circles as providing the last word in the study of biblical terms, and their authority was being too readily accepted as absolute. This is, of course, a misuse of the material, and far from representing the intentions of the authors. In these matters, new approaches and understandings continually become necessary, and, in any case, a distinction must be made between the presentation of factual material (lexical material, information about the usage of words) and the theological interpretations placed upon this. The summary to the Old Testament chapter here (pp. 31 ff.), and the many points of comment in the New Testament chapter, represent conclusions drawn by Professors Weiser and

Bultmann. But these conclusions must be carefully examined if further progress is to be made towards understanding the biblical words and ideas. A forthcoming book by Professor James Barr of Edinburgh (see the Bibliography) contains furthermore some trenchant criticism of the methods and assumptions of TWNT, and this points to the need for careful scrutiny of the evidence and its presentation.

But this is all to the good. For so central an idea as that of Faith will not readily find exhaustive treatment. The chapters of this book provide some of the material which needs to be taken into account if we are to approach an understanding of what was in the minds of biblical writers of many periods when they used words which may be reasonably translated by this word.

Reference may also appropriately be made here to Martin Buber's contrast of the 'faith of Abraham' with the 'faith of Paul' (*Two Types of Faith*, 1951), and to the discussion of this by Hans Urs von Balthasar (*Martin Buber and Christianity*, 1961).

All Hebrew words have been transliterated (unattractive though this is to the Hebraist) and, where necessary, translated. The non-Hebraist will observe that where the root of a word is cited, this is done without vowels, e.g. *'mn*, but where a particular word is mentioned, the vowels are added, e.g. *'^{e}met*. It will not normally be difficult for the connexion between different words to be recognised from the occurrence of the root letters (sometimes partly concealed as in the example just given). Four forms of the Hebrew verb are mentioned; the *qal* which is the simple form; the *niph'al* which is strictly reflexive, but often passive in meaning; the *hiph'īl* which is often though not exclusively causative in meaning; the *pi'el*, the intensive form.

Greek words are not transliterated. It is not really so very difficult for the reader with no Greek to make himself familiar with the letters, and if he will work with a Bible open, he will quickly recognise the phrases which appear in Greek here. Where quotations are given from elsewhere than the New Testament (or Septuagint) a translation has been given.

P. R. A.

CONTENTS

BIBLIOGRAPHY

General

Reference may be made to the general Theologies of the Old and New Testaments

M. Flacius: *De voce et re fidei* (1549).

H. Hoelemann: *Bibelstudien, I: Die biblischen Grundbegriffe der Wahrheit* (1859), pp. 1-53.

J. B. Lightfoot: *Epistle to the Galations* (1865, ^{10}1890), pp. 154-64. (Reprinted 1957 by Zondervan, U.S.A.)

H. H. Wendt: 'Der Gebrauch der Wörter *ἀλήθεια, ἀληθής* und *ἀληθινός* im NT auf Grund des alttestamentlichen Sprachgebrauchs', ThStKr, 56 (1883), pp. 511-47.

A. Pott: *Das Hoffen im NT in seiner Beziehung zum Glauben* (1915).

A. Nairne: *The Faith of the NT* (1920).

R. Gyllenberg: *Pistis*, I, II (Swedish) (1922).

A. Schlatter: *Der Glaube im NT* (^{4}1927).

B. B. Warfield: *Biblical Doctrines* (1929), pp. 465-508.

W. G. Kümmel: 'Der Glaube im NT', ThBl, 16 (1938), pp. 209-21.

J. Dupont: *Gnosis* (1949), pp. 250-2, 260 f., 398-409, *et passim.*

V. Warnach: *Agape* (1951), pp. 581-5 *et passim.*

C. H. Dodd: *The Bible and the Greeks* (1935), pp. 65-75.

J. Guillet: *Thèmes Bibliques* (1951) esp. chs. II, III.

P. Vallotton: *Le Christ et la Foi* (1960).

C. F. D. Moule: *An Idiom Book of NT Greek* (1953).

J. J. von Allmen: *Vocabulary of the Bible* (1958).

James Barr: *The Semantics of Biblical Language* (Oxford, to be published shortly), esp. Chapter VII on 'Faith and Truth' and the literature there discussed.

Chapter I

L. Bach: 'Der Glaube nach der Anschauung des AT', BFTh, 4 (1900), pp. 1-96.

J. Pedersen: *Israel, its life and culture*, I-II (1926), pp. 336-48.

K. H. Fahlgren: *Sedaka nahestehende und entgegengesetzte Begriffe im AT* (1932).

K. J. Cremer: 'Oudtestamentische Semasiologie', *Gereformeerd Theologisch Tijdschrift*, 48 (1948), pp. 193-200; 49 (1949), pp. 1-15, 79-99.

S. Virgulin: 'La fede nel profeta Isaia', *Biblica*, 31 (1950), pp. 346-64, 483-503.
J. C. C. van Drossen: *De derivata van den stam 'mn in het Hebreeuwsch van OT* (1951).
G. J. Botterweck: '"Gott erkennen" im Sprachgebrauch des AT', *Bonner Bibl. Beiträge*, II (1951).

Chapter II

R. Reitzenstein: *Die Hellenistischen Mysterienreligionen* (^{3}1927).
R. Walzer: *Galen on Jews and Christians* (1949), pp. 48-56.

Chapter III

W. Bousset: *Die Religion des Judentums im späthellenistischen Zeitalter*, ed. H. Gressmann (^{3}1926), pp. 193-6 *et passim*.
G. F. Moore: *Judaism* (1927-30).
H. L. Strack and P. Billerbeck: *Kommentar zum NT aus Talmud und Midrasch* i-v (^{2}1956), see iii, 187-201.
P. Volz: *Die Eschatologie der jüdischen Gemeinde im neutestamentlichen Zeitalter* (^{2}1934), pp. 80 f.

Chapter III, B, 3

H. Windisch: *Die Frömmigkeit Philos* (1909), pp. 23-29.
W. Bousset: *Kyrios Christos* (^{2}1921), pp. 145-7.
Bousset-Gressmann, pp. 447 f.
M. Peisker: *Der Glaubensbegriff bei Philon* (Dissertation, Breslau 1936).
E. Käsemann: *Das wandernde Gottesvolk* (1939), pp. 48-52.

Chapter IV, B

M. Dibelius: *Jesus* (^{2}1949), pp. 106 f.
E. Käsemann: *Das wandernde Gottesvolk* (1939), pp. 19-27.

Chapter IV, C

W. H. P. Hatch: *The Pauline Idea of Faith in its relation to Jewish and Hellenistic Religion* (1917).
W. Bousset: *Kyrios Christos* (^{2}1921), pp. 145-54.
E. Wissmann: *Das Verhältnis von πίστις und Christusfrömmigkeit bei Paulus* (1926).
W. Michaelis: 'Rechtfertigung aus Glauben bei Paulus' in *Festgabe für A. Deissmann* (1927).
E. Lohmeyer: *Grundlagen paul. Theologie* (1929).
K. Mittring: *Heilswirklichkeit bei Paulus* (1929).

M. Dibelius: 'Glaube und Mystik bei Paulus', *Neue Jahrbücher für Wissenschaft und Jugendbildung*, 7 (1931), pp. 683-99.

W. Mundle: *Der Glaubensbegriff des Paulus* (1932).

R. Gyllenberg: 'Glaube bei Paulus', ZSTh, 13 (1937), pp. 612-30.

M. Hansen: *Om Trosbegrebet hos Paulus* (1937).

R. Schnackenburg: *Das Heilsgeschehen bei der Taufe nach dem Apostel Paulus* (1950), pp. 115, 188 f., *et passim.*

Chapter IV, D

J. O. Buswell: 'The Ethics of "Believe" in the Fourth Gospel', *Biblica Sacra*, 80 (1923), pp. 28-37.

W. H. P. Hatch: *The Idea of Faith in Christian Literature from the Death of St. Paul to the Close of the Second Century* (1926).

J. Huby: 'De la connaissance de foi dans Saint Jean', *Recherches de Science religieuse*, 21 (1931), pp. 385-421.

R. Schnackenburg: *Der Glaube im vierten Evangelium* (Dissertation, Breslau 1937).

W. F. Howard: *Christianity according to St. John* ([3]1947), pp. 151-65.

C. H. Dodd: *The Interpretation of the Fourth Gospel* (1953), pp. 179-86.

ABBREVIATIONS

ATD	Das Alte Testament Deutsch (Commentary series ed. by A. Weiser, Göttingen.
BFTh	*Beiträge zur Förderung christlicher Theologie.*
BH	*Biblia Hebraica*, ed. R. Kittel (3rd edition).
Bousset-Gressmann	W. Bousset, *Die Religion des Judentums im späthellenistischen Zeitalter, ed.* H. Gressmann (^{3}1926).
EVV	English versions.
Ges.-K.	Gesenius-Kautzsch, *Hebrew Grammar.*
NGG	*Nachrichten von der Gesellschaft der Wissenschaften zu Göttingen.*
Pr-Bauer	E. Preuschen, *Griechisch-deutsches Wörterbuch . . . NT* ed. W. Bauer (^{5}1958) ET of ed. 4 (1949ff.) by W. F. Arndt and F. W. Gingrich (1957).
Str.-B.	Strack-Billerbeck, cf. Bibliography.
Theod.	Theodotion.
ThBl	*Theologische Blätter.*
ThStKr	*Theologische Studien und Kritiken.*
TWNT	*Theologisches Wörterbuch zum Neuen Testament*, ed. G. Friedrich.
VB	J. J. von Allmen ed. *Vocabulary of the Bible* (1958).
ZKG	*Zeitschrift für Kirchengeschichte.*
ZNW	*Zeitschrift für die neutestamentliche Wissenschaft.*
ZSTh	*Zeitschrift für die systematische Theologie.*

Works which appear in the Bibliography are referred to in the text and footnotes by the author's name either alone or with an abbreviated title.

I. THE OLD TESTAMENT CONCEPT

A. *General considerations*

If faith is understood in quite general terms as the relationship and attitude of man towards God, then the OT statements concerning faith do not occupy a very prominent position. Interest in man is usually overshadowed by the centrality of God. Faith as interpreted by the OT is always the response of man to the primary activity of God. In addition to this, OT religion in early times was a matter for the community[1] and it is difficult for expression to be given to the personal inner life of the community. Hence the language only begins to develop a wealth of such expressions when the individual emerges from his dependence on the community and examines the attitude of man towards God with particular interest as a result of his own inner experience. So it was the prophets who provided a fresh stimulus to the development of the language, with its wealth of metaphors treating of faith, by giving greater depth to their content; and the resources of the language available for describing faith can be found at their richest in the Psalms, where the piety of the individual has the opportunity of expressing itself most clearly.

A study of faith in the OT cannot fail to observe the striking fact that in describing man's relationship to God two fundamentally different and indeed contrasting groups of ideas are employed, namely fear and trust. The contradiction between them is felt down to a late period and yet they stand side by side and pass

[1] See Baumgärtel, *Die Eigenart der at.lichen Frömmigkeit* (1932), pp. 20-25, 49-63, 95-103.

over into each other, so that the fear of God is often simply the term for faith.[1] This tension and polarity in man's relationship to God, expressed in the antithetic quality of the words in common use, is of fundamental significance for the OT attitude to faith.[2]

The following picture is obtained by counting the number of times in which the individual groups of words are employed. The word groups denoting fear and trust to express the relationship to God are evenly balanced (they both occur about 150 times). In the case of the verbal stems of the second group, *bṭḥ* is most frequently used: it occurs 57 times in a religious sense (of which 37 are in the Psalms and 3 apply to idols), 60 times in profane usage. Next comes *ḥsh*: 34 times in a religious sense (24 times in the Psalms), 5 times in profane usage. Taking the verbs of hope, we find *qwh* 32 times referring to God (12 times in the Psalms), 11 times in profane use; *yḥl* 15 times in reference to God, 14 times in profane use, *ḥkh* 6 times referring to God, 8 times in profane use; on the other hand the *hiph'īl* of *'mn* (the LXX uses the stem *πίστις* and its derivatives for this alone) is applied directly to God only 15 times. It is combined 10 times in a religious sense with God's word, command or action, or used absolutely, besides occurring 23 times in profane usage. The *niph'al* is used 45 times, 12 times of God himself but only 3 times of the relationship of man to God.

This survey leads to the following question. Does the fact that, according to the statistics of the uses of the

[1] e.g. Gen. xx.11, xxii.12; Isa. viii.13, xi.2; Prov. i.7; Ps. xix.10, cxi.9 *et passim*.

[2] J. Hempel, *Gott und Mensch im AT* (BWANT,[2] 1936), pp. 4-33, 233-49. I intentionally avoid Hempel's expressions 'consciousness of being both at a distance and in association', because for the OT fear is more than this, namely the awareness that one's own existence is threatened and might be annihilated, and confident faith transcends association and includes a special quality of being.

individual verbal stems, the stem *'mn*—*πιστεύειν* only comes in the fourth place, give a correct picture of the qualitative weight of the individual stems in the OT? For in that case the use of *πιστεύειν* in the LXX and the NT would appear to represent an arbitrary choice of a stem of minor importance in the OT. Or, on the other hand, did not the NT after all link up with a form which was vital and fundamental for the conception of faith in the OT, and bring into prominence an expression which had been most completely and fully stamped with the depth of the OT conception of faith? None of the verbal stems named is of specifically religious origin, and their use in religion seems to have arisen out of profane roots. Consequently in order to determine their meaning we must first ascertain the particular significance of the individual verbal stems by drawing on their profane usage. We can then attempt to give a historical sketch of the changes and developments in their meaning.

B. *The root 'mn and related expressions*[1]

1. The *qal*, which occurs only as a participle, has a strictly limited range of meaning. It is used of a child's mother, nurse, attendant in II Sam. iv.4, Ruth iv.16, Num. xi.12; to denote a guardian, a foster-father in II Kings x.1, 5; Esther ii.7; (Isa. xlix.2). The passive participle in Lam. iv.5 describes the child that is *wrapped in* purple, the *niph'al* in Isa. lx.4 the child that is *carried* by its mother on her hip in the fold of her garment. The noun *'omnā* occurs in Esther ii.20 in an abstract feminine formation with the meaning of *education*, *nurture*. It is not possible to reach a definite conclusion from these passages whether the customary translation of carrying, holding, or the close association

[1] cf. *ἀλήθεια*, *truth*, in TWNT, I, pp. 233 ff. for a discussion of *'emet.*

in general between mother, nurse, attendant, guardian and the child comes nearest to the original meaning. It is just as difficult to ascertain whether there is a connexion between this employment of the word and its religious usage, and if so, what it is (cf. below, pp. 7, 11 f.).[1]

2. The range of the use of the *niph'al* is considerably wider. Its usual translation as *firm*, *certain* and *reliable* is no more than an approximation and does not represent its ultimate and fundamental meaning.[2] This can be recognised most readily in those passages in which the profane use of the verb is connected with a thing. Thus it is associated with a place in Isa. xxii.23, in order to express its suitability for a particular purpose *I will fasten it as a tent peg in a māqōm ne'ᵉmān* (*sure place*), or of a dynasty (descendants) in order to say that it will not die out (I Sam. ii.35, xxv.28; II Sam. vii.16; I Kings xi.38).[3] In Deut. xxviii.59 the participle is used for *lasting afflictions and grievous diseases* and includes not only the persistent continuance but also the devastating effect. The LXX proves that in this last case the usual translation does not cover the whole meaning, for it finds itself forced to use the paraphrase θαυμαστός (*wondrous*). In Isa. xxiii.16 the participle means the drinking water *that will not fail*; in Jer. xv.18 the *niph'al* is employed in a parallel passage as a contrast to the *deceitful brook of waters* which does not perform what it promises.[4]

[1] Nothing positive can be said about the meaning of *'ōmᵉnōt* in II Kings xviii (usually translated as *door-posts*) and about its connexion with *'mn* (? = *to carry*).

[2] The LXX translates it 29 times with πιστός, 9 times with πιστοῦν, once each with ἀξιόπιστος, ἐμπιστεύειν, πίστιν ἔχειν, and θαυμαστός.

[3] In the same sense *šālōm we'ᵉmet* I Kings xx.19 *peace and security in my days* (RSV).

[4] A similar interpretation must be given to Exod. xvii.12: *His* (Moses') *hands were 'ᵉmūnā = did not sink down*, and Jer. ii.21 where

Finally the *niph'al* is used in Gen. xlii.20 of the statement which is proved to be true because it corresponds with the facts of the case.[1] These examples show clearly that an unvarying translation with only one word is impossible[2]; thus *ne'emān* does not express a quality which is added to the subject concerned and which could equally well be attached to something else, but *'mn* is shown to be a general concept the content of which is determined differently in each case by the particular thing it describes. It declares that in any given instance the qualities to be attributed to the subject in question are actually present. Thus here *'mn* contains perhaps something which might be defined as 'specific' and means that the quality which is characteristic of the particular subject concerned is related to reality. In accordance with the OT idea of completeness this implies not only one particular

zera' 'emet=*true choice plant*, is contrasted with *nokriyyā*=*an alien, wild one.*

[1] Similarly the Aramaic passive participle *mehēmān* of the interpretation of dreams in Dan. ii.45.

[2] The difficulties which this causes in the Versions can be observed already in the LXX which adopts different methods at its several stages. The earliest—the Pentateuch and the translations influenced by it in early days, such as Isaiah in particular—give simply the appropriate meaning. The later stage which afterwards culminated in Aquila, prefers a definite equivalent for each word in the original text in order to reproduce that text as precisely (and mechanically) as possible, and then leaves the interpretation to those qualified for it (P. Katz, *Philo's Bible* (1950), especially 34 f., 42 f., 64-67, 83 ff., 149). Consequently in Exod. xvii.12 the LXX renders *yādāw 'emūnā* intelligibly with ἐστηριγμέναι, the metaphor being replaced by the concrete term, as in the Targums. On the other hand Aquila has πίστις which is not a 'literal' translation, but simply his regular word for *'emūnā*, whatever its sense may be in the context. Another example of the mechanical methods of the later translators is provided by the rendering of *'emūnā official duty* in I Chron. ix. In v. 22 *be'emūnā* is translated by τῇ πίστει αὐτῶν (cf. also vv. 26.31, Katz).

feature, but all the features taken together which pertain to this subject. Moreover the nature of the Hebrew genius demands that this relationship between concept and reality should be seen not as an abstraction of logical thought, but always as a practical experience drawn from life. Thus in the formal concept what belongs to it is conceived, felt and experienced each time together with it, and in this way the logical relationship invariably involves also a practical relationship with life. The particular meaning in any given case can be intensified or extended according to the strength of the demands or the acuteness of the power of observation.[1]

It is with these results in mind that the application of the *niph'al* to persons must be judged. It is used of a servant in I Sam. xxii.14 and in Num. xii.7 (Moses); of witnesses in Isa. viii.2, and in Jer. xlii.5 where the word expresses not only the truthfulness of the statement but includes also the capacity to observe, the understanding and the gift of description[2]; of the messenger[3] in Prov. xxv.13; of a prophet in I Sam. iii.20 where *ne'ᵉmān* is used to describe Samuel as the ideal of a prophet, 'as he ought to be'; also of a priest in I Sam. ii.35; of a city pictured as a wife in Isa. i.21, 26[4]; of officers in charge in Neh. xiii.13.[5] The conclusions reached above can without difficulty be applied to these examples, for in these too the same form of the word describes qualities quite different in themselves. The same word is used in every case because the same relationship, determined by the sense,

[1] We may perhaps think of the different characteristics which make up the concept of a genuine choice plant.

[2] cf. *'ᵉmūn* in Prov. xiv.5.

[3] *'ᵉmūn* appears for this in Prov. xiii.17; and in Prov. xx.6 of a friend.

[4] cf. Zech. viii.3 'city of *'ᵉmet*'.

[5] cf. the Aramaic passive participle, in Dan. vi.5.

exists between the qualities demanded by the conception of the subject and those which are actually present. This and the variability of the content in any given case comes out with special clarity in Prov. xi.13 where, as contrasted with the slanderer who betrays secrets, the man is *ne'ᵉman ruaḥ* whose behaviour corresponds to the meaning of a secret, namely he keeps it to himself.[1]

These examples throw light also on the religious use of the verbal stem. The nature of its form makes it possible, when it is predicated of God, for the rich abundance of the different manifestations of God's activity to be summed up in the same term *'mn*. Thus in Deut. vii.9 the *faithful* God is He who keeps covenant and *ḥesed* with those who love Him and obey His commandments, He who performs the oath which He swore to the fathers. In Isa. xlix.7 the word is used to mean the performance of God's promise to His servant with reference to his election. The *niph'al* is used to denote that God's word has come into force, has become actuality, both as a promise (I Kings viii.26; I Chron. xvii.23 f.; II Chron. i.9, vi.17; Isa. lv.3; Ps. lxxxix.29) and also as a threat (Hos. v.9)[2]; for it is part of the nature of a promise or threat that it is fulfilled. The word is employed, in a similar sense, of precepts (Ps. cxi.7) and of the law (Ps. xix.8), where in the parallel phrases *established for ever and ever*, to be performed with *'ᵉmet* and *yōšer*, *the work of his hands are 'ᵉmet and mišpāṭ*, or in the series of terms in Ps. xix, we can see that the concept includes the whole of the features which are to be expected of the law in order that it may achieve its purpose as the manifestation of

[1] In Job xii.20 *ne'ᵉmān* used absolutely denotes the well-trusted, experienced, true man, paralleled by elders and princes.

[2] In Ps. xciii.5 the *decrees* are probably meant to be understood as promises and threats.

the divine will for shaping human life. The OT speaks in the same way of God's *'emet* and *'emūnā*[1]; the basic meaning here too is the 'essential' = that which makes God to be God. The more precise definition of its content which is always in mind at the same time depends in each individual case on the particular conception of God or on that aspect of God which happens to be to the fore. Thus for example in the phrase *ḥesed we'emet*[2] or *ḥesed we'emūnā*, which became a fixed liturgical form, the word *ḥesed* (*love*, *mercy*) provides a more precise definition of its content, whilst *'emet* (*'emūnā*) (*faithfulness and constancy in His disposition and in the expression of His love*) represents the more formal element.

The *niph'al* is used of the relationship of man to God[3]: Neh. ix.8 in *thou didst find his* (Abraham's) *heart ne'emān before thee and didst make with him a covenant*, an allusion to *he'emīn* in Gen. xv.6; Ps. lxxviii.37 of the Israelites in the time of Moses *lō' ne'emenū biberītō*, to which the parallel is *their heart was not steadfast toward him*, alluding to the covenant relationship; and Ps. lxxviii.8 *lō' ne'emenū 'et-'ēl rūḥō*, referring to the disobedience towards the commandments. In these passages the idea of *'mn* expresses the attitude of man towards God which corresponds to the claim of God in the case concerned; it denotes not only the correctness of the external behaviour, but just as much the disposition, and it is not restricted to a single action performed once only, but applies to the whole of a man's relationship to God.

3. The usage of the verbal adjective *'āmēn* points in the same direction[4]; by its use in I Kings i.36 to confirm

[1] cf. p. 3, n. 1.

[2] cf. A. Weiser, *Die Psalmen* (ATD, [4]1955) 28. For *'emet* cf. the similar noun *'ōmen* in Isa.xxv.1; probably also in lxv.16.

[3] Hos. xii.1 is uncertain.

[4] Similarly the adverbs *'omnām truly* in II Kings xix.17; Isa.

a royal command; in Num. v.22, Deut. xxvii.15-26, Jer. xi.5, Neh. v.13 to accept (God's) curse; in Jer. xxviii.6 after a prediction of restoration; and implies the wish that these will be fulfilled. In Neh. viii.6; Ps. xli.13 (Heb. 14), lxxii.18, xxxix.52 (Heb. 53), cvi.48; I Chron. xvi.36, it is used as a concluding liturgical formula after a doxology. When in I Kings i.36 Benaiah replies *'āmēn* to the king's command to anoint Solomon as king, this implies that Benaiah has understood the command, agrees with it and desires that Yahweh may bring the king's word to pass, but also at the same time expresses his own obligation to contribute himself all he can to the execution of the order. Thus in *'āmēn* too the idea is present of the relationship between the claim made by the saying and its realisation, an idea which brings out the fact that all that is involved in the order (or curse, or doxology) and its consequences are to be realised. This aspect is still clearly reflected in the LXX, in which *'āmēn* is translated 14 times by *γένοιτο* and is transliterated only 3 times as ἀμήν.[1] But beside this objective connexion between idea and actual fact, we must not overlook the subjective relation of him who says *'āmēn* to that which he reinforces with his *Amen*; this includes both the subjective (theoretical) knowledge and recognition, and also at the same time the practical submission of the

xxxvii.18; Job ix.2, xii.2, xix.4 f., xxxiv.12, xxxvi.4; Ruth iii.12 and *'umnam* in questions *indeed*? Gen. xviii.13, Num. xxii.37, I Kings viii.27; II Chron. vi.18, Ps. lviii.1 (Heb. 2), and *'omnā* Gen. xx.12, Josh. vii.20.

[1] (cf. TWNT, I, 340, on ἀμήν in the NT, and Allmen VB, pp. 15 f.) In Jer. xxxv (Heb. and EVV xxviii).6 the LXX reads ἀληθῶς. In Num. v.22 and Deut. xxvii. 15-26 Symmachus and Theodotion have the transliteration ἀμήν, probably favoured by liturgical custom, whilst Aquila prefers an etymological translation, usually *πεπιστωμένως*, but in Jer. xxxv (xxviii).6 *πιστωθήτω* (so Katz privately).

whole person with his understanding, will and attitude to the obligations of the command (or curse, or doxology) in question. Thus the term *'mn*, when used in this form, comprises a double reference: the knowledge and recognition of the relation between the obligation and its realisation, and the fact that this obligation with all its practical consequences is binding on him who says *Amen.*

4. With this in mind, the *hiph'īl he'ᵉmīn to believe,*[1] rendered in the LXX 15 times as πιστεύειν, 5 times as ἐμπιστεύειν, once as καταπιστεύειν and once as πειθέσθαι, can be defined (cf. below pp. 55 f.) most simply as 'saying Amen to something with all the consequences for the subject and the object'. This expresses both that the objective relation of the idea to the object is recognised to be an actual one, and also that there is subjective connexion between the subject holding the idea and the object of it; thus when combined with the preposition *lᵉ* or with *kī* (for) (also *lᵉ* with infinitive),[2] it is rather the action itself which is emphasised, when combined with the preposition *bᵉ* it is the general attitude.[3] Thus in profane usage *to believe* a word, a report, a piece of news, means first to be aware of and to accept as true the thing reported, but at the same time it includes an attitude appropriate to the thing reported (Gen. xlv.26, Exod. iv.1, 8 f.,[4] I Kings x.7 = II Chron. ix.6, Jer. xl.14, Isa. liii.1, Hab. i.5 [Prov. xiv.15], II Chron. xxxii.15). Whilst in these cases the stress falls on the single act, the use of *he'ᵉmīn* towards persons

[1] Dan. vi.24 Aramaic *hēmīn.*

[2] The combination with *'et* (not the sign of the accusative but the preposition *with*) in Judges xi.20 should be translated *to make an agreement with . . . = to permit*; perhaps with the following infinitive construct *lᵉ* has dropped out owing to haplography.

[3] In Ps. cvi.24, cf. v.12 (also lxxviii.32), it seems as if this distinction is no longer made.

[4] Here the profane usage merges into the religious usage.

emphasises rather the basic attitude which is associated in English too with the word 'trust'. Trust with regard to the vassal (I Sam. xxvii.12), the friend (Mic. vii.5, Jer. xii.6), the flatterer (Prov. xxvi.25), the servant (Job iv.18), the holy one (Job xv.15), includes on the one hand the recognition of the claim contained in the name of friend, servant, etc., and on the other hand at the same time also the fact that this claim is binding on the man who himself trusts. Thus it is the reciprocal relationship which makes trust what it really is and not merely a one-sided connexion, that is comprised in the word *he'ᵉmīn*. Moreover the OT uses it only for a personal relationship; for also behind the word which is trusted there stands the man who is trusted.[1]

The *hiph'il* is employed analogously to express the relationship of man to God. Here too it is not used in a causative sense, but is declarative[2]: it pronounces God to be *ne'ᵉmān* or, if we may paraphrase, it says Amen to God. But even this does not embrace the whole of the meaning. Firstly in this sphere of its usage *he'ᵉmin* appears as a formal term signifying to recognise and to acknowledge the relationship into which God enters with man, i.e. to put oneself into this relationship. Thus here too the reciprocal relationship between God and man is part of the essence of faith.[3] Moreover it is

[1] Of the exceptions, Job xxxix.12: *Do you have faith in the wild ox that he will return?*, the phrase in Deut. xxviii.66 and Job xxiv.22: *to have assurance of life*, the first is probably to be understood as a metaphorical transference of a human relationship, while in the other two passages the negative meaning *there is no assurance of life* demonstrates just the impossiblity of a personal relationship to life. Perhaps too there may be an assimilation of *he'ᵉmīn* to the originally different meaning of *bṭḥ to be sure* (cf. below, pp. 19 ff.).

[2] cf. Ges.-K §53d. [Ges.-K. actually describes the declarative usage in §53c, and subsequently classifies *he'ᵉmīn* among internal Hiph'ils, in §53e. Cf. J. Barr, op. cit. on p. xi.]

[3] This meaning suggests the need to consider whether this religious usage has not its linguistic root in the concrete form

such that—even in those cases in which faith indicates a human activity for which man can be made responsible (the demand for faith)—man is never the one to initiate this reciprocal relationship. Even in passages where faith is not expressly mentioned, the assumption is always present that God is the real originator of the relationship between God and man.[1] In each individual case the manner in which the content is determined depends on the particular aspect of the reciprocal relationship which is brought to the fore. When a command, order, or commandment is concerned (Deut. ix.23, Ps. cxix.66 [II Kings xvii.14[2]]), then faith means the acknowledgement of the demand and man's obedience. When attention is concentrated on God's promise (Gen. xv.6 [Ps. cvi.12]), then *he'ᵉmīn* expresses the acknowledgement of the promise and of the power of God to perform it, and includes the honouring of God as the mighty Lord (Num. xx.12).[3] The two themes of promise and obligation seem to be combined in *he'ᵉmīn* in Exod. iv.1, 8 f. and in Ps. cvi.24.

But even this does not exhaust the range of the word. By virtue of its formal nature, *he'ᵉmīn* possesses further possibilities of being extended and deepened. These are

given in the *qal* of the relationship between the mother, nurse, etc. and the child. (cf. above, p. 3).

[1] The fact that the term *'mn* includes a reciprocal relationship seems to me still to appear in the translation of Ps. xxxi.23 (Heb. 24) where it is difficult to decide between *Yahweh preserves faith* (LXX, F. Hitzig, *Die Psalmen* (1863), ad loc.; E. König, *Die Psalmen* [1921], ad loc.) and *Yahweh preserves the faithful* (B. Duhm, 'Die Psalmen' in *Kurzer Hand. Kommentar zum AT*, 14[3] (1922), ad loc.; R. Kittel, 'Die Psalmen' in *Komm. zum AT*, 13[1,2] (1914), ad loc.; Kautzsch, ad loc.; H. Gunkel, 'Die Psalmen', in *Göttinger Hand. Komm. zum AT*, II, 2 [1926], ad loc.), according to whether the relationship is seen from the point of view of God or of man.

[2] cf. the Qumran Hab. Commentary ii.14 f.

[3] The shade of meaning in the concept of faith when faced with God's wondrous deeds in Ps. lxxviii.32.

specially directed towards including the whole relationship between God and man (Exod. xiv.31, xix.9; Num. xiv.11; Deut. i.32; Ps. lxxviii.22; perhaps already in Gen. xv.6).[1] When it is God who is in view, then all those characteristics are included which just make God to be God, and one who wishes to establish a relationship with Man: His might, His power to work miracles, His purpose in choosing His people, His disposition to love, the constancy and fidelity of His conduct, the realisation of His word and His plan, His demands, His justice; for *ḥesed*, *mišpāṭ* and *ṣᵉdēqā* are in fact frequently used in the OT to characterise the divine *'ᵉmet* more precisely. Accordingly the OT religious usage of *he'ᵉmīn* suggests the meaning of 'to take God as God with complete seriousness', and thus includes as an essential factor the exclusiveness of the divine relationship. This can also be perceived from the fact that in the language of the OT 'not to believe' is often the equivalent of 'to become an apostate' (*pš'*).[2] Since the idea of apostasy is derived from the OT ideology of the covenant and is significant only in this context, it is already apparent that the setting and origin of the religious usage of the stem *'mn* is to be sought in the OT tradition of the sacral covenant of Yahweh. Corresponding to the extensive exclusiveness there is an intensive one in so far as the term *'mn* sums up all the ways by which men express in their lives their relationship to God. Thus *he'ᵉmīn* is used with different shades of meaning. In Isa. xliii.10, when paralleled by *yd'* (*know*) and *bīn* (*understand*) *that they may believe that before me no god was formed nor shall there by any after me*, the relation-

[1] In Jonah iii.5 the heathens' faith in God (Yahweh) too must be understood to mean the whole of their religion (cf. faith in the *divine covenant* Hab. Comm. ii.4).

[2] cf. Deut. xxxii.20, where *children in whom is no 'ēmūn* has idolatry as its parallel.

ship to God is emphasised from the point of view of knowing him. In Hos. iv.1, in addition to knowledge, a strong element of emotion appears in the triad *da'at 'ᵉlōhīm, 'ᵉmet, ḥesed.* The aspect of the will is already prominent in those passages already cited in which belief is to be understood as indicating obedience. In Exod. xiv.31, Jos. xxiv.14, II Chron. xix.9, Ps. lxxxvi.11 the impulse of fear is associated with the idea of faith.[1] Similarly the fact that, in behaviour and disposition, the relationship to God excludes all others, is shown by the expression used in Hos. x.2 to describe the attitude which is the opposite of faith: *ḥālaq lēb* (probably = *to have a divided heart*), whilst conversely the phrase *with all your heart and with all your soul*, of which Deuteronomy is particularly fond (cf. Deut. vi.5 *et passim*), leaves no doubt how the OT wishes the attitude of faith to be understood. Moreover the fact that both extensive and intensive exclusiveness is a basic quality of the relationship of faith in the OT, is made clear in the passages in which it is defined more precisely with *šālēm* (*undivided* = to surrender oneself completely)[2] for here the *complete loyalty of faith* is expressed by *to follow Yahweh fully*[3] or *to be blameless before Yahweh.*[4] In all these passages there is evident a real understanding of what is meant in the OT by faith, which exhibits the course which the use of *he'ᵉmīn* has followed: a relationship to God which

[1] Isa. viii.13 *Yahweh Sabaoth, him you shall regard as holy, let him be your dread* should also be mentioned in this connexion in addition to the prophet's demand for faith. Cf. Ps. lxxviii.22 with vv. 32 ff.

[2] cf. I Kings viii.61, xi.4, xv.3, 14; II Chron. xvi.9 (with *'el*). Cf. also II Kings xx.3; Isa. xxxviii.3; II Chron. xix.9 in each case paralleled with *'ᵉmet, 'ᵉmūnā*; I Chron. xxviii.9, xxix.9 (19); II Chron. xv.17, xxv.2; frequently directed against idolatry.

[3] *millē' 'aḥᵃrē yhwh* Num. xiv.24, xxxii.11; Deut. i.36; I Kings xi.6.

[4] *tāmīm 'im yhwh* Deut. xviii.13, Ps. xviii.24 = II Sam. xxii.24 (with *lᵉ* here); as a noun parallel with *'ᵉmet* in Josh. xxiv.14, cf. I Kings ix.4.

embraces the whole man in every part of his outward behaviour and his inner life. Hence also *he'ᵉmīn* is nowhere used for the relationship with other gods, whilst *bṭḥ* and *ḥsh* are employed without hesitation in reference to idols also. This is intelligible; for only in a religion directed towards monotheism, such as the OT conception of the Yahweh covenant, is the idea of the reciprocal relationship between God and man possible with that comprehensive depth of meaning which we can discover in the usage of *he'ᵉmīn*.

It is the absolute use of *he'ᵉmīn* which exhibits its most significant development and intensification. It does so in the form which goes back to Isaiah.[1] It is the problem of how existence is possible, the question of faith and being, which is the centre of Isaiah's interest. The idea of the remnant, the hope for Zion, the founding of a religious community among his disciples—all this must probably be understood with this problem in mind and is most closely associated with the prophet's general conception of faith. This in its turn goes back to his personal encounter with God which took place within the framework of the cultic tradition (vi.1 ff.). The fact that faith is marked off from political considerations (vii.1 ff.[2]), from protection against dangers

[1] Ps. cxvi.10 may be connected with Isaiah's conception of faith. The profane usage in Job xxix.24 does not admit a similar view. The absolute usage of *he'ᵉmīn* in Isaiah has been disputed by J. Boehm, 'Der Glaube und Js.', ZAW (1923), pp. 84-93, but this view has rightly found no acceptance.

[2] This is not the place to enter into the much discussed question of the 'prophet and politics'; cf. on this in addition to the commentaries (in particular O. Procksch, *Js.*, Vol. I (Komm. AT 9), (1930), pp. 10-17; V. Herntrich, *Der Prophet Js.* (ATD 17²) (1954), pp. 11 f., 118-22); J. Hempel, 'Chronik', ZAW, 49 (1931), pp. 152 f.; F. Weinrich, *Der religiös-utopische Charakter der prophetischen Politik* (=Aus der Welt der Religion, Bibl. Reihe, Heft 7) (1932); K. Elliger, 'Prophet und Politik', ZAW, 53 (1935), pp. 3-22; J. Hempel, *Gott und Mensch im AT* (²1936), pp. 321 f.; K. Elliger,

(xxviii.14 ff.) and from reliance on human strength (xxx.15 ff.), shows, as well as the absolute use of *he'ᵉmīn*, that for Isaiah faith means an altogether special form of existence for those dependent on God alone, which becomes effective like the *might of a hero* (*gᵉbūrā*, xxx.15) and forms the foundation laid by God for the divine community[1] (xxxviii.16). In fact faith and existence are identical for Isaiah. In the well-known saying in Isa. vii.9 *'īm lō' ta'ᵃmīnū kī lō' tē'āmēnū to be established*, referring to the whole of a man's life (cf. pp. 5 f.), is thought to be not just the reward of faith, so that faith would be the prerequisite of life, but—since *kī* (surely) must be understood as both demonstrative and explicative—it expresses by this phrase that faith and *to be established* (i.e. existence) are identical. If couched in positive terms the meaning of the saying would be: the people of God have their particular manner of being and are established through their faith.[2] This

'Nochmals "Prophet und Politik" ', ZAW, 55 (1937), pp. 291-6. with an addendum by J. Hempel; H. J. Kraus, 'Prophetie und Politik', *Theol. Existenz heute*, NF. 36 (1952); E. Würthwein, 'Js. vii.1-9. Ein Beitrag zu dem Thema "Prophetie und Politik" ', *Festschrift für K. Heim* (1954), pp. 47-63. G. von Rad, *Der heilige Krieg im alten Israel* (1952), pp. 56-61, attempts to explain Isa. vii.1 ff., xxx.15 ff., xxxi.1 ff. as a vivid presentation of the early sacral ordinances of the Holy War in which he seeks the origin of the OT faith and its Sitz im Leben (cf. p. 31), but he does not do justice to the breadth of the OT conception of faith (cf. A. Weiser, review in *Für Arbeit und Besinnung*, 7 [1953], pp. 158-60).

[1] The late Jewish interpretation of the *corner-stone* as the Messiah (cf. TWNT, IV, 276) which is found in Tg Jonathan and Rashi and was accepted by F. Delitzsch, *Komm. uber das Buch Js.* (⁴1889), p. 316, and by O. Procksch, *Js.*, Vol. I (Komm. AT 9) (1930), p. 358, cannot be inferred directly from the text itself. In I Pet. ii.6 f., Isa. xxviii.16, together with Ps. cxviii.22, is applied to Christ as the corner-stone of the primitive community (cf. TWNT, VI, p. 97).

[2] Procksch does not make this quite clear in *Theologie des AT* (1950), p. 181, when he defines faith as 'the condition of existence'.

and his refusal to fear (vii.1 ff.) and to trust in any way the might of men (xxx.15 f.) which after all is transient, as well as the inclusion of the fear of Yahweh alone in the relationship of faith, shows in addition that for Isaiah faith is the only possible mode of existence, and that this utterly excludes every other independent attitude for man or any obligation towards any one other than God. For Isaiah, the only thing which matters, whatever happens or is experienced, is Yahweh, His plan and His will and the appropriate attitude of man. From this derives the exclusive character of the relationship of faith in its external aspect. So too there is perfected the inner experience of this exclusive relationship by the intimate linking of faith and existence. There can thus be no further deepening of the meaning of this word. From this point of view too Isaiah deserves to be called the prophet of faith; for he has played a decisive part in giving the ultimate depth of meaning to the content of this word, as well as causing it to influence the further development of linguistic usage.

5. A short survey of the further development of the religious use of *'mn* and its derivatives will show this. The crucial emphasis which Isaiah gave to this word and concept never dropped out of the later history of its usage. This is the main source of the strong qualitative influence of the meaning of *he'ᵉmīn* on the other roots used in the language of religion for the attitude of man towards God. Although the use of *'mn* is of less account, so far as mere numbers are concerned, the meaning of the roots *bṭḥ*, *ḥsh*, *qwh*, *yḥl*, *ḥkh*, originally very limited, merged into the sense of *he'ᵉmīn* to express the exclusive relationship of a personal nature between man and God (cf. p. 19 ff.). Where the word itself is used, there is no mistaking the tendency to stretch it to include the most comprehensive range of meaning,

just as *'ᵉmūnā* too embraces the whole attitude to life resulting from faith (Hab. ii.4,[1] II Chron. xix.9, Jer. vii.28 [v.3]).[2] Finally *'ᵉmet*, corresponding to *'ᵉlōhē 'ᵉmet*='the true God' (II Chron. xv.3), comes to denote true religion altogether (Dan. viii.12, ix.13, x.21)[3] and thereby finally the idea of exclusiveness issues in a claim to be absolute.

6. One question remains to be answered. Whence came that strong religious impulse which by means of the stem *'mn* gave expression to the peculiarity of OT religion at its various stages? It seems to be connected from the beginning most closely with the particular character of the religious set-up and of the development of thought in the Israelite religion of Yahweh. In the 'Succession History of David', written by a contemporary, the old saying has been handed down in II Sam. xx.18 f.[4]: *Let them but ask at Abel and Dan whether what the 'ᵉmūnē yisrā'ēl ordained has fallen into disuse.* The intention is to reproach Joab with wishing to destroy the 'heritage of Yahweh' by laying siege to Abel. The fact that in this passage the designation the *faithful ones of Israel* has been preserved in an old proverb and is brought into a pertinent connexion with the religious and dogmatic concept of the 'heritage of Yahweh' suggests the conclusion that the original home of this

[1] In the original prophecy in Hab. ii.9 (see BH) *the righteous* means the congregation. It was only by the change of the prophecy into a proverb, which occurred already in OT times, that the particular interpretation 'a pious individual' arose. It is this which underlies Paul's quotation in Rom. i.17 (cf. *Righteousness* in this series, pp. 46 ff.), Gal. iii.11 (ibid., p. 24, 62). The LXX ὁ δε δίκαιος ἐκ πίστεώς μου ζησεται presupposes *be'ᵉmūnātī*, i.e. God's faithfulness to his covenant, and by this change-over to the theocentric outlook the word is given another meaning.

[2] On *'ēmūn* in this sense cf. Deut. xxvii.20.

[3] Similarly perhaps in Ps. xxv.5, xxvi.3, lxxxvi.11.

[4] According to the LXX which has preserved a better text here.

old usage of *'mn* was in the association of the Yahweh Covenant and its sacral tradition. Thus from the beginning the particular way in which the Israelites developed the Yahweh religion seems to have shaped the religious tone given to the term *'mn* in the OT. It is true that in the ordinary usage the more general term *bᵉrīt* prevailed to denote the special relationship between Yahweh and Israel,[1] and not until Neh. ix.38 (x.1 in Heb.) is *'ᵃmānā* used to describe the declaration by which the covenant was renewed in the religious reform of Nehemiah.[2] But the fact that the majority of the passages in which the OT uses *he'ᵉmīn* refer to the relationship to God of the Mosaic period (Exod. iv.8 f., xiv.31, xix.9; Num. xiv.11, xx.12; Deut. i.32, ix.23; II Kings xvii.14; Ps. lxxviii.22, 23, cvi.12, 24) after all shows clearly enough the close connexion between the special meaning of the term *'mn* and the sacral tradition concerning the beginnings of the Yahweh religion in Israel. The OT saw in the relationship described by *he'ᵉmīn* the special religious attitude of the people of God to Yahweh.[3] This is all the more significant since this attitude provides the pattern according to which the OT religion was again and again regenerated and developed.

C. *The root bṭḥ*

1. In the case of *bṭḥ*, which the LXX translates mainly with πεποιθέναι and ἐλπίζειν, the position is the reverse of that of *he'ᵉmīn*. The English 'to trust' is richer in meaning than the original meaning of the root. The

[1] On the 'covenant' cf. TWNT, II, pp. 120 ff., J. Pedersen, *Israel*, I-II (1926), pp. 263-310.

[2] cf. the use of *'ᵉmūnā* for the duties of those entrusted with the service of the temple cult in I Chron. ix.22, 26, 31.

[3] The use of *he'ᵉmīn* in Gen. xv.6 does not contradict this, for in the perfect type of Abraham who believed, the author has given us a sketch of his own ideas of faith from the post-Mosaic time.

basic significance can still be recognised clearly in its absolute use, especially in the early passage in Judges xviii.7, 27, where *bōṭēaḥ* (*unsuspecting*) is explained by *šōqēṭ* (*quiet*) and in v. 7 by *yōšebet lābeṭaḥ* (*dwelling in security*) (LXX: ἡσυχάζειν); thus *bṭḥ* means *to be in a state of security* (*beṭaḥ*). We find that in Judges xviii and in Prov. xi.15 (LXX ἀσφάλεια) (Job xl.23) the objective state is emphasised, whilst in Isa. xxxii.9-11, xii.21; Jer. xii.5; Ps. xxvii.3; Prov. xiv.16, xxviii.1; Job vi.20, xi.18 the subjective feeling of security, usually contrasted with fear, is emphasised.[1] As contrasted with *he'ᵉmīn*, *bṭḥ* expresses, even when the means or the author of the security is added with the prepositions *bᵉ*, *'al* or *'el*, not a relationship but the condition, corresponding perhaps most nearly to the translation: *to feel secure by reason of* . . . (or *to base one's security on* . . .). This is evident from passages where *bṭḥ* is used of confidence in a man's own resources (Ps. xlix.6 [Heb. 7], Prov. xxviii.26), his own achievement (Hab. ii.18, Jer. xlviii.7), his own righteousness (Ezek. xxxiii.13) or in reference to such things as ambushes (Judges xx.36), chariots (Hos. x.13 [LXXA], Isa. xxxi.1), cities (Amos vi.1; Jer. v.17), walls (Deut. xxviii.52), bows (Ps. xliv.6 [Heb. 7]), riches (Jer. xlix.4, Ps. lii.7 [Heb. 9]; Prov. xi.28), beauty (Ezek. xvi.15), oppression (Isa. xxx.12, Ps. lxii.10 [Heb. 11]), wickedness (Isa. xlviii. 10), and where there can be no question of a reciprocal relationship as in the case of *'mn*. Even where the word is connected with persons, it appears from some earlier passages, especially where it is used with *'al* (II Kings

[1] Similarly *mibṭāḥ* = 'basis, originator of security' (in the LXX 9 times ἐλπίς 3 times πεποιθέναι) especially in Isa. xxxii.18; Prov. xiv.26; *kesel* = confidence Ps. xlix.13 (Heb. 14) (LXX has σκάνδαλον); Job xxxi.24, viii.14 (*kislā* Job iv.6; LXX ἀφροσύνη); in ritual language it has still preserved its original meaning = 'loins' in Lev. iii.4, 10, 15 *et passim.*

xviii.20, 24) and with the ethical dative (II Kings xviii.21, 24 [Jer. vii.4, 8]), that here a subjective feeling of safety attributed to the individual must be distinguished from the concepts of relationship described by *'mn*. The passive participle *bāṭūaḥ b^{e}yhwh* too, *made safe by Yahweh* (Ps. cxii.7, Isa. xxvi.3) as well as the *hiph'il*: *Do not let Hezekiah make you rely on ('el) Yahweh* (II Kings xviii.30[1]) shows the same meaning of the stem. To this must be added the frequent use of the word in a derogatory sense in the prophets in order to express and to attack man's self-reliance (of the 30 cases in which *bṭḥ* is used of things, 20 are found in the prophetic writings; as many as 11 in Jeremiah, yet only once with a positive meaning, in xxxix.18). The fact that *'mn* can never denote confidence in idols, whilst *bṭḥ* does so without hesitation (Isa. xlii.17, Jer. xlvi.25), may provide evidence for the difference between the meaning and use of *bṭḥ* and that of *'mn*.[2]

2. Yet beside the use of *bṭḥ* meaning *to feel oneself secure* we may note an extension of meaning in its religious usage, namely in the direction of assimilating it to that of *he'^{e}mīn* (Jer. xxxix.18, Zeph. iii.2 (Mic. ii.5)). This occurs especially often in Deuteronomy, where no difference is any longer made between *bṭḥ* and *he'^{e}mīn*. In later additions to the prophetic literature also, *bṭḥ* has acquired the meaning of a term for relationship, even where occasionally the original meaning of the objective feeling of security is still dimly visible (Isa. 1.10, Jer. xlvi.25[3]). This process goes so far that—above all in the Wisdom literature and in the Psalms—

[1] cf. Ps. xxii.9 (Heb. 10).

[2] Parallel with this *smk* = *to be stayed on*, in the passive participle of the *qal* in Isa. xxvi.3, Ps. cxii.8; in the *niph'al* in Ps. lxxi.6 (Isa. xlviii.2); the *niph'al* of *š^{e}n* in profane usage in Isa. xxx.12, xxxi.1; Job viii.15, and in religious usage in Isa. 1.10 (II Chron. xiii.18, xiv.11 [Heb. 10], xvi.7 f.; Mic. iii.11).

[3] Here the translation *to rely on* would really be most appropriate.

bṭḥ meaning *he'ᵉmīn* has almost completely ousted the latter. Thus for example in Prov. iii.5 *trust* in Yahweh *with all your heart* is spoken of just as though it were faith. In Ps. lxxviii.22, xxxvii.3 *bṭḥ* and *he'ᵉmīn* (*'ᵉmūnā*) are used in parallel. In Ps. xl.3 (Heb. 4), lvi.4, xxvi.1, 3 fear is also included in the whole relationship to God. Further in those cases in which there is no direct parallel to *he'ᵉmīn*, *bṭḥ* is used quite commonly for the *pious man* generally (Prov. xvi.20, xxviii.25, xxix.25; Ps. xxxii.10, cxxv.1; Jer. xvii.7); often also in the well-worn form for the attitude of prayer in liturgical opening and closing formulae (Ps. xci.2, lxxxiv.12 [Heb. 13], xxv.2, xxxi.6 [Heb. 7], *et passim*). The development of the usage here follows a line similar to that of *'mn*.

3. Since the development of the meaning of *'mn* took place without a change in its basic sense, the alteration of meaning of *bṭḥ* when compared with it requires an explanation. In general terms the following factors may be regarded as effective forces in the linguistic transformation: the evolution of the monotheistic faith in Yahweh in the tradition of the Yahweh cult, an evolution which asserted itself more and more definitely in its struggle with alien religions, the influence of the prophets and the pressure of history, the religious situation during the exile and political impotence also in the post-exilic period, the growing feeling of *being cast on God* (for this expression see Ps. xxii.10 [Heb. 11]), which seeks and finds its security in God alone. Besides these we may note the development of religious individualism, through which, in connexion with the transformation of the nation into a religious community, the piety of the laity called forth by the prophetic movement gains more and more ground. Moreover a decisive turning point in the use of *bṭḥ* for the whole attitude to faith may be fixed even more precisely. It arises from the influence of Isaiah on the shaping of

religious language, which can be illustrated from the significant passage in Isa. xxx.15. Isaiah too is well aware of the use of *bṭḥ* in the sense of man-made objective security (xxx.12, xxxi.1, xxxii.9 ff.), which he attacks; but in xxx.15 he employs the verbal stem with a positive meaning: *In returning* (*šūbā*) *and rest* (*naḥat*) *you shall be saved, in quietness* (*hašqēṭ*) *and trust* (*biṭḥā*) *shall be your strength* (*g*ᵉ*būrā*). The fact that Isaiah does not choose a form of the verb *bṭḥ* but creates two fresh formations, *biṭḥā* and *šūbā*[1] perhaps reveals his intention of distinguishing this word clearly from the meaning which he has rejected in other passages. In any case we can see here clearly his struggle to find language in which to express a content which represents something new as compared with the previous meaning of *bṭḥ*. It is true that in this passage too the old meaning of *feeling secure* can still be detected, but both *šūbā* (*returning*) and *g*ᵉ*būratkem* (*your strength*) enable us to see beneath them the concept of faith of Isa. vii.9, xxviii.16, and what follows—*And you would not, and you said 'No. We will speed upon horses'*—shows clearly that *strength* here does not mean their own strength, but that which issues from the relationship with God (*biṭḥā*). At this point we can put our finger directly on the change of meaning: Isaiah filled the verbal stem with the content of his own concept of faith and by his creative action here too, as in the case of *'mn*, gave a fresh stimulus to the development of the verbal usage.

D. *The root ḥsh*

1. *Ḥsh to seek* (*find*) *refuge, to make oneself safe*[2] (the

[1] Both these formations occur only here in the OT. [Ed. It must, however, be observed that an argument based on hapaxlegomena is never entirely satisfactory.]

[2] cf. *refuge ḥāsūt* in Isa. xxx.3; *maḥ*ᵃ*seh* in Ps. civ.18; Job xxiv.8; Isa xxviii.15 in profane use (LXX καταφυγή, σκέπη, ἐλπίς); used of

Accadian *ḫisu* has the same meaning; in the LXX 20 times ἐλπίζειν, 9 times πεποιθέναι, 3 times εὐλαβεῖσθαι twice σκεπάζειν, once each σῴζειν and ἀντέχειν) shows a development similar to that of *bṭḥ*. It belongs to a somewhat more elevated style and compared with *bṭḥ* its original range of meaning is rather more restricted. For whilst *bṭḥ* can also mean self-reliance, based on one's own strength (cf. p. 20), *ḥsh* presupposes rather being dependent on protection and in need of help. The poetic root-meaning can still be seen in the use of the word in the simile of the tree in the shadow of which one *takes refuge* (Judges ix.15, Isa. xxx.2) *to take refuge in the protection of Egypt*; or in the simile of a bird with outstretched wings *under whose wings one takes refuge* (Ruth ii.12; Ps. xxxvi.7 [Heb. 8], lxi.4 [Heb. 5], xci.4). Moreover the second simile is found applied only to Yahweh. The primary meaning here too is not to be thought of as a reciprocal relationship between the one who seeks and the one who bestows protection, but the objective state of being protected or the action which seeks to reach such a condition. This is just as evident from its connexion with *taḥat* (*under*) (Ruth ii.12, Ps. xci.4), as from the phrase *finds refuge through his integrity* (Prov. xiv.32).[1] Like *bṭḥ* (cf. p. 21) *ḥsh* can also be applied to gods (Deut. xxxii.37).

2. As an expression for the relationship with Yahweh, *ḥsh* has also often still preserved the colouring of its original meaning, especially in the Psalms where the worshipper in all kinds of temptation and danger seeks his God (Ps. lvii.1 [Heb. 2], xci.4, xxv.20, lxi.4 [Heb. 5] *et passim*). But often—and this suggests the comparison with *bṭḥ*—especially in the opening and closing for-

Yahweh in Ps. xlvi.1 (Heb. 2), lxi.4, xc.9 *et passim* (LXX καταφυγή, ἐλπίς).

[1] Read with the LXX Syr *bᵉtummō* instead of *bᵉmōtō* (in his *death*.

mulae of the liturgy, the word has become hackneyed in use and its meaning has been extended to the whole relationship to God (Ps. vii.1 [Heb. 2], xvi.1, xviii.2 [Heb. 3], xxv.20, xxxi.2, ii.11 [Heb. 12], v.11 [Heb. 12], xxxiv.22 [Heb. 23]). It is used in parallel with *bṭḥ* in Ps. cxviii.8 f. [cf. xxv.2 and 20] and parallel to *fearing God* in xxxi.19 [Heb. 20]). The final stage of this linguistic development seems to be the absolute of the *qal* participle *hōsīm* meaning *the godly* (Ps. xvii.7[1]). The same tendency is seen in the extension of the meaning of *maḥseh* which was used originally of the *security*, of the *place* and the *giver of protection* in Ps. lxii.7 (Heb. 8), xciv.22; in lxxiii.28 *I have made Yahweh my refuge* is paralleled with *being near God* and is applied to the actual relationship to God. The depth of meaning in the word here does not fall short of Isaiah's concept of faith (cf. p. 28.)[2]

E. *The roots qwh, yḥl, ḥkh*

An essential part of the OT attitude of faith, namely that part of it which looks toward the future, could not

[1] Yet the LXX adds ἐπὶ σέ.

[2] In a certain sense the development of the verbs *drš* and *bqš* (*to seek*) might be compared. They were originally restricted to religious usage in questions addressed to the divine oracle (Gen. xxv.22; I Sam. ix.9; I Kings xxii.8; II Kings xxii.13, 18; (to Baal) II Kings i.2 f., 6, 16; to a soothsayer in I Sam. xxviii.7; to the dead in Isa. viii.19, Deut. xviii.11), and also to seeking the face of the deity in the cult (II Sam. xxi.1; Ps. xxiv.6, xxvii.8, cv.4; Hos. v.[6], 15 [II Sam. xii.16, Zeph. i.6]), and finally as the expression of the whole relationship to God including its inward aspects, e.g. Amos v.4, Deut. iv.29 *to seek with all your heart and with all your soul*; similarly Jer. xxix.13; then as a participle frequently describing the godly generally, e.g. Ps. ix.10 (Heb. 11), xl.16 (Heb. 17), lxix.6 (Heb. 7) *et passim.* The fact that the prophets rejected the externalised worship of the cult and made the relationship with God deeper and more spiritual seems here too to have been the decisive factor in this change of meaning.

be appreciated if the stems of the verbs of hope[1] were not taken into account. They must be brought into the investigation of faith for another reason also, namely that in later times they are used in the OT in exactly the same sense as the verbs of believing. In spite of the fact that the basic meaning of the individual stems is different, a common treatment of this group of words is justified because the development through which they passed was similar, and also because the three stems often appear simply as alternatives. This is brought out by their being translated with the same words expressing *hope*, *waiting for*.

1. The basic meaning of these words is the concrete condition of tension. *qwh*, of which the stem is attested with the same meaning in Accadian, Arabic and Syriac and which has preserved its original meaning most clearly in *qaw*, *a measuring line*, and in *tiqwā* (Joshua ii.18, 21), *a twisted cord*, means in the first instance *to be stretched*. *yḥl* seems to be connected with *ḥīl to be in labour*, *to give birth to*.[2] This would also explain the stronger expression of feeling which is still noticeable in the later use of this verb; the basic meaning is *the state of painful expectation*. *ḥkh* seems to have preserved its fundamental sense most clearly in II Kings ix.3 where it means *to restrain oneself*, *to hesitate*, and probably also in Hos. vi.9 to express *tense lying in wait* (in a hostile sense).

In profane usage the original meaning also still shows through; thus *qwh* is used in Job vii.2 of the workman *who looks for his wage* or in Ps. lvi.6 (Heb. 7), cxix.95

[1] cf. *Hope* (ἐλπίς), to be published shortly in this series.

[2] Grammatically this may be a case of the tendency in the imperative and infinitive of the verbs beginning with *y* to represent an enlargement of the stems with two radicals into stems of three radicals. For this tendency cf. G. Beer, *Hebr. Grammatik*, II (1921), p. 42.

they *lie in wait to destroy me*. The painful undertone of waiting can still be heard in *yḥl* in I Sam. xiii.8 where we are told that Saul *waited* seven days in vain for Samuel, or in the saying of Job xiv.14 *I would wait all the days of my service*. In each of these cases the subjective condition of waiting stands in the forefront of the meaning. Both of these last-named stems have their original meaning expanded, especially in Proverbs and Job where they are often used with the general sense of *vital hope* (*vital energy*), and this usage reveals clearly the influence of reflexion on the concept (*qwh*: Job iii.9, xxx.26[1]; *yḥl*: Job vi.11, xiii.15, xxx.26[2]).

2. In religious usage the verbs of hope are found first as the expression of the tension of looking to a definite goal, and in fact when used collectively of the godly usually with reference to the hope of salvation, frequently in the metaphorical phrase *hoping for light*: *qwh* in Jer. viii.15, xiii.16; Isa. lix.9, 11, lxiv.3 (Heb. 2); in Jer. xiv.19 paralleled with *ḥkh*; *yḥl* in Ezek. xiii.6; *ḥkh* in Zeph. iii.8; Ps. cvi.13. In the case of individual godly men, it means hope for divine help in any kind of trouble, in prayers with reference to waiting to be heard, thus especially in Ps. cxix.81: of the hope of God's salvation; in vv. 74, 114, 147: of hope in God's word; in v. 43, in God's ordinances; in Ps. xxxiii.18, of His love. In the case of *qwh*, although Yahweh himself is named everywhere as the object of hope, yet sometimes a quite definite expectation lies behind this *hope in Yahweh*. Thus in Prov. xx.22 the hope for help, in Ps. xl.1 (Heb. 2) for prayer to be heard. It is probably the same in Ps. cxxx.5 as a parallel to *yḥl* and in Ps. xxxiii.20

[1] cf. the abstract feminine formation *tiqwāh* with the same meaning in Prov. xxiii.18, xxiv.14, xxvi.12, xxix.20; Job v.16, viii.13, xi.18, 20, xiv.7, xvii.15, xix.10, xxvii.8; *miqweh* I Chron. xxix.15.

[2] cf. *tōḥelet* as a parallel to *tiqwāh* in Prov. x.28, xi.7.

where the three verbal stems *ḥkh*, *bṭḥ* and *yḥl* are used side by side in a similar sense.[1] The last-named passages do indeed show a usage, namely the waiting for God himself, which cannot be simply regarded as a direct transference of the basic meaning to the religious sphere. The root of this linguistic form, which occurs most commonly in the Psalms, may perhaps have lain in the expectation of a theophany, perhaps during the cult, perhaps in world events, as announced particularly by the prophets. From there the usage may have passed through Deutero-Isaiah[2] to that eschatological use which we meet in later Judaism and which is found in Dan. xii.12 *Blessed is he who waits . . . to the end of the days* (*ḥkh* Theod. *ὑπομένειν* cf. Matt. x.22, xxiv.13; Mark xiii.13). And in all passages in which hope in God includes a definite goal, the pronounced this-worldly character of OT piety with its particularly intense interest in the visible appearance of the divine rule, would seem to express itself in the form of a theophany of the kind already mentioned.

3. But besides this, yet another development emerges which has transformed *hope for God* into a distinct expression of faith as a general relationship to God. In fact, here too, as in the case of *'mn* (cf. pp. 15 ff.) and *bṭḥ* (cf. pp. 22 f.), it is Isaiah in whose writings there becomes apparent the decisive change of meaning in the verbs of hope towards their final depth of meaning in the OT. Isa. viii.17 shows us the prophet in an attitude of faith before the hidden God: *I will wait* (*ḥkh*) *for Yahweh who is hiding his face from the house of*

[1] The verb *śbr* is also used similarly (*qal*=*examine carefully* in Neh. ii.13, 15) in the *pi'el*=*hope* in Ps. civ.27, cxlv.15 in the sense of waiting on God as the giver of food, in Ps. cxix.166 of hope for help, in Isa. xxxviii.18 for hope of God's *'emet*; cf. the noun *śēber hope* for God's help, in Ps. cxlvi.5.

[2] Isa. li.5 *the isles* (RSV *coastlands*) *wait for me* (*qwh*) (lx.9); xlii.4 (*yḥl*) seems to mean 'waiting for the manifestation of God'.

Jacob and I will hope in him (*qwh*). The change we find here becomes plain when it is contrasted with II Kings vi.33. Here the king (Joram?) says to Elisha with regard to the famine in Samaria: *This trouble is from Yahweh! Why should I wait for Yahweh any longer* (*yḥl*)*?* The difference is evident: the moment in which the king gives up hoping for Yahweh becomes for Isaiah the very moment in which he dares to 'hope' more than ever. The judgement and anger of God did not, it seems, interrupt for him the relationship with God which had existed up till then. Isaiah's faith continues to endure, but it endures—and this is the new factor in his realisation of faith in which the original meaning of *qwh* and *ḥkh* still shows through—in a tension, in a state when the strength of his faith is strained to the utmost, in the background of which the tension between fear and hope can be felt. This waiting and hoping is a faith which does not see and yet believes. The tension in the soul of the prophet, expressed in the basic meaning of the words *qwh* and *ḥkh*, springs from his knowledge of the tremendous daring of such a faith in view of his desperate external situation. It is not resignation with the faint ray of hope of a 'perhaps', but the heightened strength of a 'nevertheless', achieved after the ultimate struggle for certainty, that lies embedded in this 'tension' of faith.

No one understood the real depths of these struggles of Isaiah for faith better than Deutero-Isaiah, to whom we owe in Isa. xl.31 the classical formulation of the OT hope of faith. His conception is born out of a similar spiritual situation and points in the same direction: he too is concerned with the hidden God. Under the influence of their downfall in the exile, the people believe themselves to be forsaken by God (xl.27): *My way is hid from Yahweh and my right is disregarded by my God.* Deutero-Isaiah snatches these weary souls—and

in this we see the same 'nevertheless' as in Isaiah—from the brink of their despair by pointing to just this hidden God, to his unfathomable wisdom and his inexhaustible strength which he grants precisely to the helpless (vv. 28 f.). It is in this situation that he coins the saying *they who wait* (*qwh*) *for Yahweh shall renew*[1] *their strength* (v. 31). Here the 'hope in Yahweh' is recognised to be a new kind of existence and vital energy, a superhuman miraculous power which makes possible the impossible: the youths may be weary and faint and the young men may break down (v. 30, note the stylistic hyperbole!). He who waits for Yahweh can run and not grow weary. Here is expressed clearly the difference between physical life-force and the vital energy of faith as a (spiritual) force of a different kind, which confesses God in the face of all appearances and in this relationship with God overcomes all temptations and weakness. Deutero-Isaiah too knows this further truth and thereby associates himself most closely with Isaiah's conception of faith (cf. xxviii.16) that it is God himself who bestows on man such strength through faith (cf. xl.29). The whole of Deutero-Isaiah's prophecy, including the song in chapter liii, is the living proof of the victorious power of the strength of faith, which overcomes in man's soul the most dire misfortunes of this life on earth and even death itself, because its roots lie in another, transcendent world.

4. An extension and intensification of the verbs of hope in the direction indicated by its use by the two Isaiahs can be observed also in later passages and especially in the Psalms. In addition to the usage already mentioned in the sense of hope for particular aid or for answer to prayer and beside the strong emotional tinge of longing, the word 'to hope' is em-

[1] *ḥlp pi'el* and *hiph'il* = *replace, change* (of clothing) in Gen. xli.14, II Sam. xii.20.

ployed especially in the Psalms for the whole position with regard to man's relationship with God in general, as e.g. Ps. xlii.5 (Heb. 6), 11 (Heb. 12), xliii.5: *Hope* (*yḥl*) *in God, for I shall again praise him, that he is the help of my countenance* (see BH) *and my God* (cf. Ps. cxxx.5 f.). In the course of this development the verbal stems of hope are used as synonyms of *bṭḥ* (Ps. xxv.3, 5, cf. v. 2, xxxiii.21 f.),[1] of *ḥsh* (Ps. xxv.21 cf. v. 20), and of *yr'* (*to fear*, cf. v. 14; xxxiii.22 cf. v. 8), without the possibility of establishing any difference in meaning. The apparently almost playful ringing of the changes in Ps. cxix[2] on the most varied verbs for the relationship to God is probably the clearest evidence for the fact that the linguistic usage in the OT flows through the most diverse tributaries into one main stream. What has been observed already in the case of the other verbal stems is confirmed also in the verbs of hoping, namely that at last they become stereotyped formulae and describe the attitude of the godly worshipper—especially in liturgical forms in Isa. xxxiii.2: *qwh*; in Ps. xxxiii.22, cxix.147: *yḥl*; in Isa. xxx.18; Ps. xxxiii.20 *ḥkh*—or denote the godly in general as contrasted with the wicked in Ps. xxxvii.9.

F. *Summary*

If the development of OT usage as a whole is surveyed in the light of this study, the answer can be given to the question posed at the beginning: the LXX and the NT did after all see matters essentially correctly when they attached their concept of faith (πιστεύειν) to the OT stem *'mn*. For this is the one which brings out the peculiar quality and also the most profound thought in what the OT has to say about faith. Although if

[1] The case is the same when Yahweh is described as 'the hope' of the worshipper in Ps. lxxi.5; *tiqwātī* as a parallel to *mibṭāḥī*.

[2] cf. for this especially *to hope* in vv. 43, 49, 74, 147.

mere numbers are taken into account *he'ᵉmīn* is of less importance than other verbal stems, yet there is no doubt of its qualitative preponderance. This can be recognised from the notable fact that it is one of the most significant features of the linguistic development of the other verbal stems that they become assimilated to the meaning of *'mn*, involving a more or less pronounced change in their meaning. There are three reasons for this remarkable process. (1) Linguistically the root *'mn* shows itself to be by nature a concept of very wide range and flexibility as regards its meaning; thus it is able to admit more and more fresh elements without giving up its basic meaning. So in the *hiph'il* it includes the comprehensive, exclusive and personal reciprocal relationship between God and man. (2) Historically this meaning of the *'mn* concept came nearest to the peculiar connexion with God, that of Yahweh and Israel, and probably became already in early days the expression of that specifically OT relationship with God which was fostered in the covenant tradition. (3) Theologically the prophetic movement, especially Isaiah, through personal religious experience and meditation reached the ultimate depths of this relationship to God and of the knowledge of its nature, and gave to the usage a creative intensity and—within the range of OT thought—a completeness which was taken up by the piety of individuals and helped again and again in the inward mastering of historical catastrophes and personal troubles.[1] For the significance of the OT concept of faith lies in this, that it is the expression of the particular form of existence and

[1] The objective vividness felt from the beginning to be more definitely inherent in the stems *bṭḥ*, *ḥsh*, *qwh*, *yḥl*, *ḥkh* as compared with the term *he'ᵉmīn* may have contributed to the fact that these stems, especially after their meaning had become assimilated to that of *'mn*, outstripped the use of the latter numerically.

life of the people of God and of its members, who stood in an active relationship with God; that it embraces this relationship in its whole wide range and penetrates to its utmost depths. For these come into view only when, under the threat to human existence, divine assurance releases fresh forces of faith and life.

II. THE LINGUISTIC USAGE IN GREEK

A. *Classical usage*[1]

Amongst the words formed with *πισ-τ-* the earliest attested is the verbal adjective *πιστός* with its privative formation *ἄπιστος*. It includes active and passive meanings *trusting* and *trustworthy* (*reliable*). In Homer only the latter sense appears; but since *ἄπιστος* is found there in the sense of *mistrustful* (e.g. *Od.* 14.150), it is clear that both these meanings are originally inherent in the word. They are both found again too in the noun *πίστις*.

1. In the literature we meet with *πιστός* with the meanings (*a*) *trusting* (Theogn. 283); it is used in poetic language of trust in weapons, or in skill in their use (Aesch. *Prom.* 915-17, *Pers.* 52-57); of trust in man (Theogn., and also Soph. *Oed. Col.* 1031, Dio C. 37.12.1). In so far as trust can be a duty, *πιστός* can acquire the nuance of *obedient*. (*b*) *πιστός* in the sense of *trustworthy* is to start with a word used in the sacral and juristic sphere; *oaths* are designated as *πιστά* (Hom. *Il.* 2.124 etc.), similarly *proofs* (Aesch. *Suppl.* 53, etc.). The expression *πιστὰ διδόναι καὶ λαμβάνειν* signifies *to make a covenant*.[2] *Τὰ πιστά* is the *reliability* of those bound by the covenant (Aesch. *Ag.* 651; Xenoph. *An.* II.4, 7), *loyalty*; similarly *τὸ πιστόν* (Thuc. I.68.1). It is in keeping with this that *πιστός* (*trustworthy*, *loyal*) is used of persons who are connected with one another by a

[1] This chapter includes a discussion of only those principal meanings of *πίστις* etc. in Greek literature which are important for the history of the biblical concept or for a comparison with it.

[2] Xenoph. *An.* III.2.5, IV.8.7 etc. Also as late as P. Petr. II.19.1, 4 (third century B.C.): *τά πιστὰ διδόναι* *to give a firm guarantee*.

covenant[1]: the companion, the friend, the husband, the witness and the messenger, the guard and the slave, and others too are characterised as *πιστός*, and similarly the wife as *πιστή*. The meaning becomes generalised, so that *τὸ πιστόν* can signify *reliability* and *security* in general,[2] and that *πιστός* becomes the name for the quality of *loyalty* in general. *Πιστός* is not used of things in the strict sense, but only of people and of circumstances which are brought about by people or endured by them. The *reliability* of things is denoted by *βέβαιος* which can become partly synonymous with *πιστός* because it can be used also for persons and personal behaviour.[3] In special cases a word can be described as *πιστός*; and so too the tongue, so that in philosophy the *λόγος* (Plat. *Tim.* 498), the hypothesis (Plat. *Phaed.* 107b) or the proof (Plat. *Phaed.* 245c) can be called *πιστός*, and *πιστός* may be combined with *demonstrable* (ἀποδεικτικός) (Arist. *Rhet.* II.1, p 1377 b 23).

2. The meanings of *ἄπιστος* correspond to this: (*a*) *Mistrustful*, Homer (*Od.* 14.150 *et passim*) and frequently later. (*b*) *Disloyal*, *unreliable*, already in Homer and frequently thereafter. The unreliability of circumstances, like that of persons, can also be denoted by *ἄπιστος* (Thuc. I.120.4), and so too particularly the word or speech (Hdt. III.80; Plat. *Phaedr.* 245c). In this way *ἄπιστος* acquires the meaning of *unworthy of belief*.

3. Corresponding to the usage of *πιστός*, *πίστις* has (*a*) the (abstract) meaning of *trust*, *confidence*[4] and in fact

[1] cf. especially Xenoph. *Hist. Graec.* II.3.29. On a Syrian inscription *πιστός* appears simply as the designation of a *confidant*, see Lietzmann, *Komm. z. 1 Kor.* (vii.25).

[2] Occasionally *πιστός* can also mean *genuine*.

[3] On *βέβαιος* cf. TWNT, I, p. 600.

[4] cf. Hes. *Op.* 372; Theogn. 831; Soph. *Oed.* 950. The nouns in -*τις* (-*σις*) are originally *only* abstract; what are evidently concrete meanings must somehow be derived from them.

in this sense can be applied to circumstances (Thuc. I. 120.5) and to things (Plat. *Phaedr.* 275a) as well as to persons. Trust, in so far as it contains a factor of uncertainty which can be contrasted with knowledge (Soph. *Trach.* 588-93), can nevertheless also mean *conviction* and (subjective) *certainty*.[1] Parmenides contrasts πίστις ἀληθής (Fr. 1.30 [Diels, 7th ed., I.230.12]) *reliable truth* (literally: trust in what is real) with human opinions. Plato also speaks of the πίστις μόνιμος (*well-established belief*, *Rep.* VI.505e) and of opinions and beliefs which are assured and true, but which must nevertheless be distinguished from perception and knowledge (*Tim.* 37b, c). Similarly he contrasts right belief with knowledge (*Rep.* X.601e). But often the meaning of πίστις is *firm conviction* without any such distinction. (*b*) In accordance with the genius of the Greek language, πίστις can mean both the *trust that a man feels* as well as the *trust that he inspires*,[2] that is to say *trustworthiness*. This meaning is related to that of *reliability* (cf. p. 35), but must be carefully distinguished from it. It resembles rather that of the passive form πιστεύεσθαι. It is often emphasised that πίστις is a higher good than riches. (*c*) When used in a concrete sense πίστις means the *guarantee* which makes it possible to feel trust, that *which is reliable* (or the *assurance of reliability*). Here too we find at first the sacral and juristic usage. It stands for *plighting troth*, the *pledge of faithfulness*, *becoming bail* (Soph. *Oed. Col.* 1632, *Trach.* 1182 f.). From this point πίστις can on the one hand gain the meaning of *certainty*, *credibility* (e.g. Aristot. *Eth. Nic.* X.9, p 1179 a 17 f.), and on the other that of *evidence*, *proof* (e.g. Democr. Fr. 125). It denotes in

[1] So explicitly in Plato. Cf. especially *Rep.* VI.511e. For the Platonic concept of πίστις cf. J. Stengel, *Plato als Erzieher* (1928), p. 233: the word πίστις in the subject index.

[2] cf. on δόξα, TWNT, II, p. 237.

particular the reliability of persons, *loyalty* (e.g. Aesch. *Pers.* 443). It is mentioned especially as an attribute of friendship (e.g. Xenoph. *An.* I.6.3).

4. *Πιστεύω* (in use only from the seventh century) is derived from *πιστός* and means to *trust*, to *rely on*.[1] Treaties and oaths are objects of *πιστεύειν* (Xenoph. *An.* III.1.29, V.2.9), also laws (Aeschin. *Oratio in Ctesiphum*, 1); then means of power, such as military equipment (Polyb. 5.62.6) or in the abstract: the state of reliability (Demosth. *Or.* 44.3) or the possibility of it (Plat. *Rep.* X.603b); finally persons (e.g. Thuc. III.83. 2) and in this case *πιστεύειν* can receive the shade of meaning of to *obey* (e.g. Soph. *Oed. Tyr.* 625). The passive *πιστεύεσθαι* means to *be trusted* (e.g. Xenoph. *An.* VII.6.33). In so far as words can be the object of *πιστεύειν* (e.g. Hdt. II.118), it acquires the meaning of to *believe*, and can in this sense have a person as an object (in the dative, e.g. Hdt. II.120) or a thing (in the accusative, Aristot. *An. Pri.* II.23, p 68 b 13). But it can also be construed with *περί* (e.g. Hdt. IV.96) or with the accusative and infinitive (e.g. Hdt. VI.105), or with a clause with *ὅτι* (Plat. *Gorg.* 512e), and it can also be used absolutely, but in such a case an object is to be supplied (e.g. Soph. *Oed. Tyr.* 625). In the sense of to *believe*, it can also be used in the passive (Plat. *Leg.* I.636d; Aristot. *An.* III.3, p 428 b 4), and the dative personal object may in the passive construction become the subject (Xenoph. *An.* VII.7.25). In later times it often means to *entrust* (e.g. Plut. *Apophth.*: *Agis junior*, 2 [II.191e]) which is still rare in Attic Greek (e.g. Thuc. II.35.1); it is frequently so used in the passive (e.g. Polyb. 8.17.4).

5. The privative formation *ἀπιστέω*, derived from *ἄπιστος*, is apparently not attested with the meaning to *be untrustworthy*, *unreliable*; on the other hand it is found

[1] cf. E. Fraenkel, *Griech. Denominativa* (1906), p. 179.

with that of to *be suspicious*, *mistrustful*, *incredulous* (e.g. Hom. *Od.* 13.339). In this sense it is applied particularly to words (Eur. *Med.* 927) and can mean therefore *not to believe* (Epict. II.22.23; Plot. *Enn.* V.8.11, p 246.2 ff.). The passive can also be used in this way (Xenoph. *Hier.* 4.1). The meaning to *be disobedient* has branched off from this (e.g. Hdt. VI.108), particularly when laws are the subject of πιστεύειν (Soph. *Ant.* 219, 381 f., 655 f.)

6. The noun belonging to it, ἀπιστία, means: (*a*) *unreliability*, *disloyalty* (Soph. *Oed. Col.* 611; Xenoph. *An.* II. 5.21, III.2.3) and hence *untrustworthiness* (Hdt. I.193; Plat. *Phaed.* 88d). (*b*) *Distrust*, *disbelief* (Theogn. 831).

7. Amongst additional formations with πιστ-, in view of the NT, πιστόω must also be mentioned.[1] It means: (*a*) to *make someone* πιστός, that is to say a person bound to oneself by an oath, a treaty, bail, or similarly, and therefore reliable (Soph. *Oed. Col.* 650; Thuc. IV.88). In this sense it is also used in the passive (Hom. *Od.* 15. 436; Eur. *Iph. Aul.* 66). In the middle voice the meaning becomes to *give* (*mutual*) *pledges of fidelity* (Hom. *Il.* 6.238, 21.286; Polyb. 1.43.5, 18.22.6). (*b*) to *inspire confidence in a person*. In this sense the passive is used: to *be rendered trustful*, to *feel confidence* (Hom. *Od.* 21.217 f.; Soph. *Oed. Col.* 1039).

8. We must observe that the formations with πιστ- did not become technical terms of religious language in classical Greek. It is true that faithfulness to one's word is also a religious duty (Xenoph. *Ag.* 3.5) and loyalty and piety are closely linked (Eur. *Hec.* 1234 f.). Moreover πίσυνος, which is synonymous with πιστός in the sense of *relying on*, can have the deity as its object (Aesch. *Sept. c. Theb.* 211 f.) and ἄπιστος = *unbelieving* can also be directed towards a deity (Eur. *Iph. Taur.* 1475 f.). But in no sense was πιστός used to denote the really

[1] cf. E. Fraenkel, op. cit. (p. 37, n. 1), p. 150.

religious relationship to God or the fundamental religious attitude of man.

Nor did *πίστις* become a technical term in religion; the most that can be said is that such a possibility was prepared for by the fact that *πίστις* in the sense of *reliance upon* can refer to a divine oracle (e.g. Soph. *Oed. Tyr.* 1445) and that in the sense of *conviction* can also have the existence of a deity as its object (Plat. *Leg.* XII.966d). Only the beginnings of a religious usage are to be found in the cases of *πιστεύειν*, *ἀπιστεῖν* and *ἀπιστία*. *Πιστεύειν* in the sense of to *trust* can be applied to the divine favour (*τύχη*, e.g. Thuc. V.104), and also to the deity (e.g. Aristoph. *Nu.* 437). When it means to *give credence to* the object can be both the works of man and divine oracles (e.g. Aesch. *Pers.* 800 f.), but also the deity itself (Soph. *Phil.* 1374). The same is true also for *ἀπιστεῖν* and *ἀπιστία* (e.g. Hdt. I. 158).

B. *Hellenistic usage*

1. *The development of a religious usage in philosophical discussion*

Whilst in the early Greek world it is customary to express the belief that there are gods by the word *νομίζειν* (Aesch. *Pers.* 497 f.), in later times *πιστεύειν* can also be said instead, in accordance with the fact that *πιστεύειν* may acquire the meaning to *believe* (cf. p. 37).

This linguistic usage is developed in the discussions against scepticism and atheism (cf. Plut. *Superst.* 11 [II.170 f.]). The belief that gods exist has its own proper certainty, but it is not at all self-evident and presupposes an obstacle to be overcome. The fact that divine control of the world is invisible must not be an

obstacle to believing in it.[1] Thus man must be educated by knowledge to believe in the incorporeal, for the instrument (or author) of faith cannot be sensual perception, but only the mind (cf. Plot. *Enn.* V.8.11, p 246. 2 ff.). The deity itself under certain circumstances leads the unbeliever to belief.[2] This makes it clear that *πίστις* is not only a theoretical conviction, but at the same time piety. Similarly belief in God is also belief in divine providence (cf. Plut. *Ser. Num. Pun.* 3 [II. 549b]), and the pious quality of such belief is emphasised by Plutarch (*Pyth. Or.* 18 [II.402c]). Porphyry describes how this belief determines the attitude to life (*Marc.* 21 ff.). Belief in the invisible includes also belief in the immortality of the soul (Plot. *Enn.* IV.7.10, p 138.6 ff.), even the belief that one forms part of the divine world oneself (Plot. *Enn.* IV.8.1, p 142.10 ff.) and further the belief in a judgement after death.[3] Hence it is intelligible that *πίστις* is reckoned by Porphyry (*Marc.* 24) as one of the four elements (*στοιχεῖα*).[4]

[1] Pseud.-Aristot. *Mund.* 6, p 399 b 21 f. But cf. already Heracl. Fr. 86 (Diels, 7th ed., I.170.5 f.): 'the knowledge of the divine is for the most part concealed from the understanding because there is no belief in it' (so Diels, 2nd ed., I.74.34 ff.); cf. Plut. *De Coriolano* 38 (I.232c), who refers to the statement of Heracl., when speaking of the *πίστις* in the wonderful quality of the power (*δύναμις*) of God.

[2] Vett. Val. IX.1, p 331.12 f.: 'Life, the deity, comes to him who has discerned law in the vicissitudes of life; it is denied to him who has not discerned it.'

[3] cf. Scott I.366.6 ff.: 'the *incredibilitas humana* despises the belief in a judgment after death, but the *incredibiles . . . post delicta cogentur credere, non verbis, sed exemplis, nec minis, sed ipsa passione poenarum* (Scott I.366.20 f.).

[4] Similarly in the *Orac. Chald.*, *πίστις* with truth (*ἀλήθεια*) and love (*ἔρως*) forms a triad (W. Kroll, 'De Oraculis Chaldaicis', *Breslau Philologische Abh.* VII.1 [1894], p. 26).

2. *The language of religious propaganda*[1] *and of Stoicism*

The use of πίστις as a technical term in religious language was encouraged further by the fact that it became the key word in the propaganda of the proselytising religions, not only Christianity. Every missionary sermon demands 'belief' in the deity it proclaims.

Thus Celsus says that some (the Christians) preach this saviour, others that one, but that they all say: *believe* (πίστευσον) *if you wish to be saved, or refuse* (Orig. *Cels.* VI.11). The Hermetic writings reflect this usage (e.g. *Corp. Herm.* 4.4). The mind as it follows the word of the sermon is raised to the truth and thus attains to belief.[2] Thus Lucius who has been instructed in the mysteries of Isis confesses *I now took part in the divine worship, full of that confidence* (*plena fiducia*) *which my knowledge of a kindred religion produced.* (Apul. *Met.* XI.28). This usage is also presupposed in the Litany of Isis (P. Oxy. XI.1380.152) in words which can only mean either 'who invoke thee as befits the relationship of belief (between God and man)' or 'according to the manner of believers'.[3] The Odes of Solomon show the same usage: 'Mercy is manifested for your deliverance. Believe and you will live and be delivered.'[4] In the sphere of belief in miracles and dogmas πιστεύειν etc.

[1] cf. Reitzenstein, *Hell. Myst.* pp. 234-6; O. Kitzig, *Die Bekehrung des Paulus* (1932), pp. 176-80.

[2] *Corp. Herm.* 9.10; unfortunately the text is not quite certain; cf. Scott I.185.25-186.4 and Reitzenstein, *Hell. Myst.* p. 235.

[3] cf. R. Reitzenstein, 'Die Formel Glaube, Liebe, Hoffnung bei Paulus', *NGG Philologischhist. Klasse* (1917), p. 132.

[4] Od. Sol. 34.6; cf. also 4.5, 8.11, 28.3, 29.6, 35.5, 13; and the 'believers' in 4.3, 15.10, 22.7. Naturally it is not possible to determine how far the mention of belief in Mandaean and Manichaean literature has its origin in the general religious history of Hellenism and how far Christian usage is at work here. Cf. H. Jonas, *Gnosis und spätantiker Geist*, I (^{2}1954), p. 137 and the material collected in Wissmann, pp. 44 f.

is found in the Pythagorean legend[1]; and finally this terminology penetrated also into magic.[2] It must remain an open question whether the 'Virgin of Faith' who according to an Aramaean inscription is taken to wife by 'King Bel', is to be understood in this sense. 'The Virgin of Faith' seems to be a personification of the Mazdaean religion.[3] The title of the Gnostic work 'Pistis Sophia' is evidence for the mythological personification of *Πίστις*, but this may go back to Christian usage.[4]

In Stoicism too, *πίστις* has no religious significance in the sense of denoting the relationship of a man to the deity, so that the deity and his rule should be the object of *πίστις*. But the attitude of *πίστις* is certainly a religious attitude in so far as man, if he is *πιστός* or the like, expresses in it his relationship to God.

[1] Jamblichus, *Vit. Pyth.* 138, p 78.17 ff.; 148, p 83.18 ff.

[2] cf. Preis, *Zaub.* I.4.1012 ff.; XII.288 f.

[3] M. Lidzbarski, *Ephemeris*, I (1900), p. 69; Reitzenstein, *Hell. Myst.*, p. 235; H. Gressmann, 'Das religionsgeschichtliche Problem des Ursprungs der hell. Erlösungsreligion', ZKG, NF 3 (1922), p. 186.

[4] C. Schmidt, *Pistis Sophia* (1925), p. xxi; cf. the personification of *Πίστις* in the inscription of Aberkios (cf. F. J. Dölger *Ichthys* II (1922), pp. 482 f.); Ign. Sm. x.2 where Jesus Christ Himself is designated *ἡ τελεία πίστις* (or *ἐλπίς*).

III. FAITH IN JUDAISM

A. *The Old Testament heritage*

THE *he'ᵉmīn* of the OT (cf. pp. 10 ff.) is rendered in the LXX almost without exception by *πιστεύειν*[1] and in fact corresponds to the Greek *πιστεύειν* in so far as, like the latter, it means *to trust* (in persons in I Sam. xxvii.12, Mic. vii.5 etc.), *to put trust in* (words in Gen. xlv.26, I Kings x.7, Prov. xiv.15 etc. cf. p. 37). Further the meaning to put one's trust in God (Gen. xv.6, Deut. i.32 etc.) and the fact that it is God's words which are 'believed' (Ps. cvi. 12, 24) corresponds to the Greek use of *πιστεύειν* (cf. pp. 38 f.). However what is denoted by *he'ᵉmīn* and therewith the OT concept of faith, has a richer content than that described in Greek by *πιστεύειν* and the Greek concept of faith. Although the shade of meaning 'to obey' can also be inherent in the word *πιστέυειν* (cf. pp. 34, 37 f.), yet this element is very much more prominent in 'to believe' in the OT and is often the predominant one. When referring to the relationship with God, *he'ᵉmīn* often has the meaning of 'to acknowledge' (Exod. xiv.31, Num. xx.12, Isa. xliii.10) or 'to obey' (Deut. ix.23, Num. xiv.11, II Kings xvii.14; similarly with reference to Moses, the representative of God, in Exod. iv.1, 8 f.); hence God's commandments also can be the object of *he'ᵉmīn* (cf. p. 12).

In the OT to believe in God means also to acknowledge him to be God (cf. pp. 11 f.); this includes both trust (cf. pp. 19 ff.) and hope (cf. pp. 27 f.) as well as fear (cf. p. 14) and obedience (cf. p. 12). But these two together form a unity, because trust is given a fundamen-

[1] See Additional Note, pp. 55 f.

tal sense (cf. p. 15) and embraces both the conquest of fear as well as of self-confidence.[1] To believe is the daring decision for God when a man renounces the threatening world as well as his own strength (cf. p. 17). It is therefore—and occasionally this is emphasised (e.g. Gen. xv.6)—faith against appearances and 'as a trustful decision for God it involves suppressed temptation'.[2] Such faith in God is not a general 'trust in God', but is founded on what God has done in the past.[3] It is therefore always closely related to the past and thus is at the same time loyalty (cf. p. 14).

He who trusts (*ma'^{a}mīn* = *πιστεύων*) is at the same time one who is loyal (*ne'^{e}mān* = *πιστός*). By analogy faith is closely related to the future (cf. p. 12); it is the certainty that God will do what he has promised. Its opposite is murmuring and doubting (cf. TWNT, I, pp. 729 ff., II, pp. 97 ff.) by which God is 'tempted'; it is hoping expectantly (cf. pp. 28 f. and also p. 26, n. 1) and being still. It is also closely related to the present, as being obedience to God's commandments (cf. p. 12) since by keeping them the nation must demonstrate its loyalty to the covenant.

Faith of this kind applies essentially in the OT to the history of the nation whose existence is founded on God's action and whose obedience God demands. Therefore actually the individual practises faith in so far as he is a member of the nation; his faith is directed towards the future of the nation.[4] Now it goes without

[1] This fundamental manner of understanding the concept has of course not been developed in every case: cf. especially Isa. vii.4-9, viii.5-15, xxviii.15 f., xxx.15-17 and the Psalms.

[2] cf. Schlatter, *Glaube*, pp. 10 f.

[3] Thus faith is not an attribute of a man's character, like *πίστις* in Stoicism.

[4] Abraham's faith too in Gen. xv.6 does not concern his personal fate, but the future of the nation whose ancestor he is. His faith is a prototype.

saying that faith in God, corresponding to the completeness of God's claim on the nation, must determine its life in every respect and not only occasionally in particular circumstances. But—compared with the standard of the NT—it is also evident that the OT is not yet aware of faith as that attitude which dominates the life of a man absolutely, as can be seen for instance by the fact that the question of death is not brought within the range of the idea of faith. Where in the Psalms trust in God is voiced concerning the fate of an individual (cf. pp. 30 f.), one aspect only of this faith is meant, namely trust in God's help, especially in times of distress. This can already be seen from the fact that in these cases the word used is not *he'ᵉmīn* which associates faith with history, but *bṭḥ*, *qwh* and others.[1] Thus man's position is not conceived basically as one of insecurity in the presence of God, with the implication that a man can stand before God relying neither on his good deeds nor on his bad ones, but only on his 'faith', that is on a complete abandonment of himself, and that all his doings can have no value in God's sight except in so far as they spring from faith (Rom. xiv.23). In fact it is often the case that the claim to trust is founded on a man's piety[2] which is therefore not understood completely as faith.

Finally, in the OT, God's activity, to which man knows he is committed by his loyalty and on which he trustfully places his hope for the future, is understood to be an activity of this world, whether it takes place in the history of the nation or in the fate of the individual.

[1] It should be noticed that no noun connected with *he'ᵉmīn* has been found to correspond for example with *mibṭāḥ* or *tiqwāh* although *'ᵉmet* in the sense of loyalty can to a certain extent be considered as a substitute. Only in Aramaic was a noun formed from this with the meaning of loyalty and faith, cf. Schlatter, *Glaube*, pp. 559 f.

[2] e.g. Ps. xvi, xxxvii, lii, lxxi.

Therefore although faith, by its renunciation of both fear and self-reliance, implies a turning away from the world, yet it is not the radical attitude of casting off the world, like the NT πίστις; for with this faith the εἰρήνη πρὸς τὸν θεόν (Rom. v.1) is proof against the national history on this world's stage and against the fate of the individual in this life.

B. *The concept of faith in Judaism*[1]

The OT heritage was taken over as their own jointly by Palestinian as well as by Hellenistic Jewry. Consequently it is hardly possible to differentiate here between the two trends; only particular features within the general treatment may occasionally be brought out, and Philo must be treated separately.

1. *The Old Testament motifs*

The structure of the Jewish concept of faith (which needs to be presented here only according to its religious, and not its profane usage) exhibits the leading motifs of the OT throughout: faith is trusting (cf. pp. 19 ff.) just as much as believing; it includes loyalty (cf. p. 14) and obedience (cf. p. 12) just as much as hoping and expecting (cf. pp. 27 f.). Because these motifs have an underlying connexion, it often cannot be discerned which of them is predominant. Yet it is noticeable that in the rabbinic literature faith is understood onesidedly as obedience to the law, whilst in the Apocrypha and Pseudepigrapha the other motifs contained in the structure as a whole are more prominent.[2]

The idea of loyalty often stands out.[3] It applies to

[1] cf. Schlatter, *Glaube*, pp. 9-42; Bousset-Gressmann, pp. 190-201; Moore, II, pp. 237 f.; Wissmann, pp. 50-54; A. Meyer, *Das Rätsel des Jakobusbriefes* (1930), pp. 123-41.

[2] Str.-B. III, p. 188.

[3] Schlatter, *Glaube*, pp. 15 f. So also in the Qumran texts:

the 'covenants' of God (II Esdras iii.32). It must be preserved in affliction.[1] Faith will triumph[2]; *for he who believes will gain his life in truth* (Syr. Bar. liv.16). *Great in the sight of God is loyalty to faith.*[3] This quality is probably also meant when works and faith are combined (II Esdras ix.7, xiii.22). Abraham and other patriarchs are considered to be examples of such loyalty.[4] Loyalty has to prove itself particularly in temptation, as in the case of Abraham.[5] At the same time loyalty is obedience and so occasionally the law, the commandments, are named as objects of faith.[6] In the rabbinic literature too 'to believe in God' and 'to obey God' are synonymous.[7] Hand in hand with obedience we find trust. Keeping the law (*nṣr* LXX πιστεύειν) and trusting God (*bṭḥ* LXX πεποιθέναι) appear as parallels.[8] Naturally there are many sayings in which faith is praised as trust in God[9] and men are exhorted to trust in God when in distress and in time

Manual of Discipline viii.3, x.25; *Hab. Comm.* viii.3. Here it is everywhere *'ᵉmūnā* whilst *'ᵉmet* seems to have throughout the meaning of 'truth'; and this appears perhaps also in the phrase '*āśā 'ᵉmet* (*to act truly*) i.5, viii.2.

[1] IV Macc. xv.24, xvi.22, xvii.2; Slav. En. lxii.1, lxvi.6; Ex. R. xv.7 (in Schlatter, *Glaube*, p. 17); Tg J I on Isa. xxviii.16 (in Meyer, op. cit. (p. 46, n. 1) p. 130; cf. Schlatter, *Glaube*, pp. 17 f.; Str.-B. III, pp. 192 f.

[2] II Esdras vii.34; other references in Str.-B. III, p. 193.

[3] Mekhilta Exod. xiv.31 and xv.1 (in Meyer op. cit. [p. 46, n. 1], p. 130).

[4] Sir. xliv.20; Jub. xix.9; I Macc. ii.52; IV Macc. xvi.22; Str.-B. III, pp. 199 ff.; Moore, II, pp. 237 f.

[5] Sir. ii.1 ff.; Judith viii.25 ff.; Ps. Sol. xvi.14 f.; cf. A. Sommer, *Der Begriff der Versuchung im AT und Judentum* (Diss. Breslau, 1935), pp. 12-15.

[6] Syr. Bar. liv.5, II Esdras vii.24; cf. Schlatter, *Glaube*, pp. 19 f.

[7] Str.-B. III, p. 191.

[8] Sir. xxii.24; cf. xi.21; Syr. Bar. xlviii.22; in the Greek text of Sir. xxxiii.3 the law actually takes the place of God.

[9] I Macc. ii.59; Jos. *Ant.* 3.309, 20.48; cf. Moore, I, pp. 136 f.

of trial.[1] Faith in divine providence is a specifically Hellenistic phrase used for such trust in God (Jos. *Ant.* 4.60; *Ap.* 2.170). The antithesis of faith—both in the sense of loyalty and of trust—is the doubt which tempts God,[2] distrust.[3] On the other hand a characteristic of faith is simplicity,[4] the single-minded aim of the heart. This is demanded in the XII Testaments as the opposite of double-mindedness,[5] which Rabbinic literature also attacks.[6] Associated with this is the concept of the man of little faith,[7] and also that of the hypocrite.[8] In so far as trust in God is faith in his promise, it is at the same time hope.[9] But in so far as it looks into the future in general, it is in a more universal sense belief in retribution[10] and in so far as retribution is thought of as in the hereafter such a faith becomes a party matter (cf. G. F. Moore, *Judaism*, II (1927), pp. 279 ff.).

To hold that something is true, which is of the essence of faith, when its object is originally God's word and promises,[11] acquires in the controversies with other religions and in propaganda a special meaning; belief

[1] Sir. ii.1 ff.; Jos. *Ant.* 2.333; cf. Meyer, op. cit. p. 46, n. 1), 131; Str.-B. III, pp. 191 f.

[2] Judith viii.12 ff., Wisd. of Sol. i.2; cf. Sommer, op. cit. (p. 47, n. 5), pp. 11 f.

[3] Wisd. of Sol. i.2.

[4] Wisd. of Sol. i.1.

[5] Bousset-Gressmann, pp. 418 f.

[6] Schlatter, *Glaube*, pp. 18 f.; Str.-B. III, p. 751 on Jas. i.8; Hauck, *Jakobusbrief* (1926), p. 49, n. 47.

[7] *qᵉṭannē ʾᵃmānā*, cf. Str.-B. I, pp. 438 f.; cf. especially Sota 48 b: 'He who has bread in his basket and says "What shall I eat tomorrow?" belongs to the men of little faith', (cf. p. 62).

[8] Schlatter, *Glaube*, p. 19.

[9] Syr. Bar. xlii, lvii.2, lix.2, 10; II Esdras vi.5; cf. the linking of believing and hoping in I Macc. ii.59, 61; Sir. ii.6, 8 f.

[10] Str.-B. III, pp. 190 f.

[11] Tobit xiv.4, Wisd. of Sol. xviii.6, Tg J I on Isa. vii.9 (the words of the prophets).

in God becomes a confession of monotheism.[1] Naturally this meaning of faith is especially developed in Hellenistic Judaism (Sib. III.584 ff.). Thus we find in Philo (cf. pp. 52 ff.), sentences which seem to approximate to credal formulations (Philo. *Op. Mund.* 170-2, *Virt.* 216) and the first Mandate of Hermas also goes back to such a tradition.[2]

Since 'faith' is used so broadly to express the relationship of man to God and to his law, and consequently the attitude of the pious, it is easy to understand that words denoting faith can also be used absolutely. It is true that faith is usually qualified by the addition of its object (God, God's testimonies, and so forth).[3] But the absolute usage is also found. The pious can be described simply as the 'faithful',[4] and also as the 'believers' (II Esdras vii.131). The development of this usage evidently came about in order to contrast them firstly with the 'ungodly' amongst their own nation[5] and secondly with the heathen.[6] Analogously 'faith' is also employed absolutely.[7]

[1] Judith xiv.10; Eth. En. xliii.4, xlvi.4 f. etc.; cf. Str.-B. III, pp. 189 f.

[2] Herm. m.I.1. Cf. Dib. *Herm.* ad loc.; Windisch on Jas. ii.19; cf. Wissmann, pp. 49 f.

[3] Schlatter, *Glaube*, p. 20 A 1: 'It is instructive that the Targum is no longer able to accept the absolute usage of Isaiah, but supplies faith with an object in the words of the prophet.'

[4] Schlatter, *Glaube*, pp. 15 f.; Str.-B. III, p. 189; I Macc. ii.52; perhaps also Wisd. of Sol. iii.9 (cf. next note).

[5] Wisd. of Sol. iii.9 (if *πιστοί* here does not mean the 'pious'); II Esdras vii.131; Syr. Bar. xlii.2, liv.16, 21; Slav. En. li.2; rabbinic references in Str.-B. III, p. 189.

[6] Eth. En. xlvi.8; Sib. III. 69, 724, V.161, 426; cf. I Macc. ii. 59; Wisd. of Sol. xviii.13; cf. Str.-B. III, p. 189.

[7] Wisd. of Sol. iii.14 f.; Mekhilta Exod. xvi.19 (Schlatter, *Glaube*, p. 21); Tg J I on Isa. xxviii.16 (in Meyer, op. cit. [p. 46, n. 1], p. 130); Ass. Mos. iv.8; II Esdras vi.27, vii.34, ix.7; Eth. En. lviii.5, lxi.4, 11; Slav. En. lxii.1, lxvi.6; Syr. Bar. lix.10; Sib. III. 585; Test. L. viii.2. In the inscriptions in the Jewish catacomb on

To sum up it may be said that though the concept of faith in Judaism contains the same leading ideas as that of the OT, yet there is a great difference between them.[1]

2. *How the faith of Judaism differs from that of the Old Testament*

In consequence of the canonisation of tradition in the 'scripture', obedient loyalty acquires the character of obedience to the Law, i.e. it is no longer really loyalty toward the activity of God experienced in history whilst trusting in his future activity in the same sphere.

History is, as it were, suspended and a real sense of being bound up with it is lacking. The significance of the past history is restricted to making the Jew conscious of the fact that he belongs to the called and chosen people. The present can no longer actively carry on history and its tradition, but is a medium for conveying only the canonised tradition. The text of the scriptures, accepted as belonging to a timeless present, is appropriated and interpreted by theological and legal study. Faith loses its character as a decision at a particular time in a historical situation, and 'therefore presents itself as something objective and persistent, as a form of consciousness, which having entered into the teaching

Monteverde 145: *quae vera fides* (N. Müller, *Die Inschriften der jüdischen Katakombe am Monteverde zu Rom* [1919], p. 134, or J. B. Frey, *Corpus Inscriptionum Judaicorum*, I [1936], no. 476; cf. also nos. 72 and 641).—The expression 'men of faith' is also found, cf. Str.-B. III, p. 189, in Heb. En. these 'men of faith' appear to be a circle in which apocalyptic mysteries are handed down. Cf. perhaps also the Qumran texts; cf. H. Bardtke, *Die Handschriftenfunde am Toten Meer* (1952), p. 93 n. 4. Cf. also Wissmann, pp. 40-43.

[1] Schlatter, *Glaube*, p. 12: 'For the inner form of faith depends on what is presented to us in history as the act and gift of God. The divine gifts which Jewry in NT times knew that it possessed were the Bible and the Temple. From this knowledge sprang the differences between the attitude to belief of the Judaism contemporary with the NT and that of pre-exilic times.'

of the scriptures may be experienced in them'.[1] The conception of the inspiration of the scriptures limits the working of the spirit to the past[2] and limits the divine activity to the historical events of the past. As a result there arises a 'disparagement of the natural conditions of life',[3] and faith, in so far as it nevertheless hopes that God will act, is directed to one object only, namely miracles.[4] In consequence, trust no longer applies to their historical destiny, in which the nation and individuals are involved by what they do; but is essentially a matter of resigning oneself to suffering,[5] and a belief in providence of a general nature, or the expectation of miracles. Hope looks beyond history to the supernatural eschatological events and God's judgement is no longer thought of as being carried out in historical happenings, but as eschatological action in a court of law. In the same way the figure of the Messiah as hoped for in the early days can be transformed under the influence of the figure of the 'Son of Man' or even be supplanted by it.[6] Salvation is no longer to be bestowed upon the future generations of the nation, but upon the faithful and the pious. Judgement will become a universal judgement and faith with regard to the future will become in the main belief in individual retribution, itself lacking in confidence.[7]

Belief in retribution is at the same time belief in merit. The faithful obedience to the law leads to obedience to the letter and to counting as merit the

[1] Schlatter, *Glaube*, p. 20. [2] Schlatter, *Glaube*, pp. 14 f.

[3] Schlatter, *Glaube*, pp. 22 f. The question whether it is compatible with faith to consult a doctor is an indication of this.

[4] Schlatter, *Glaube*, p. 25.

[5] This is particularly impressive in Akiba, cf. Schlatter, *Glaube*, pp. 45-48.

[6] [cf. on this whole question S. Mowinckel, *He that cometh*, E.T. by G. W. Anderson (1956), esp. Part II.]

[7] Schlatter, *Glaube*, pp. 32-35.

commandments which have been fulfilled. This presupposes that man is free in a way contrary to the freedom of genuine faith.[1] Man does not throw himself completely on God's mercy and so God's mercy and his condemnation to punishment diverge.[2] Mercy is understood to be merely leniency which overlooks individual offences; the 'righteous' man is in no need of mercy; only he who is 'converted' receives it[3]; the righteous man relies on his own merit. By placing faith beside works it is recognised that there is an obedience of faith which is not simply satisfied by the righteousness of a man's works, but which means submission to the divine will as a whole. But this insight loses its value because faith itself is considered meritorious.[4]

3. *Philo's concept of faith*

Philo's description of faith places him within the framework of Hellenistic Judaism, since faith means for him primarily faith in the one God and trust in his providence. Both are summed up in *Virt.* 216: 'And, therefore, he is the first person (i.e. Abraham, cf. Gen. xv.6) spoken of as believing in God, since he first grasped a firm and unswerving conception of the truth that there is one Cause above all, and that it provides for the world and all that there is therein.' When speaking of trust in God's help[5] and of his promises[6]

[1] Schlatter, *Glaube*, p. 26: 'By his act man substantiates God's act.'

[2] Schlatter, *Glaube*, p. 40: 'Divine forgiveness . . . is not all of a piece, and so cannot embrace the single personality and the totality of its history and unite it with God.'

[3] Schlatter, *Glaube*, pp. 38 f.

[4] For the conception of the meritoriousness of faith see Schlatter, *Glaube*, pp. 29-32. Meyer op. cit. (p. 46, n. 1), p. 132; Str.-B. III, pp. 199-201.

[5] *Sacr. AC* 70; *Vit. Mos.* I.225, II.259.

[6] *Leg. All.* III.308; *Mut. Nom.* 166; *Abr.* 275.

Philo echoes the words of Judaism as a whole.[1] But the real meaning of faith consists for him in the fact that faith is turning away from the world of birth and death and turning towards the eternal God, by which man finds the security for which he is continually searching. Philo has therefore understood man's relation to God in terms of the Greek and Platonic tradition. Yet at the same time he holds fast to the meaning of *trust* as the basic significance of *πίστις*. He says for example: 'To trust God is a true teaching, but to trust our vain reasonings is a lie' (*Leg. All.* 229, and cf. 222 ff.); or: 'Now he who has sincerely believed in God has learned to disbelieve in all else, all that is created only to perish' (*Praem. Poen.* 28); or: 'But he to whom it is given to gaze and soar beyond not only material but all immaterial things, and to take God for his sole stay and support with a reasonableness whose resolution falters not, and a faith unswerving and securely founded, will be a truly happy and twice blessed man' (*Praem. Poen.* 30). The turning towards God is not indeed the response to God's word, that is to say, to his activity in history, but it is the result of contemplation of the world[2] and is an attitude of the mind ('dispositions', *Conf. Ling.* 31), a virtue, indeed the 'most perfect of virtues' (*Rer. Div. Her.* 96), the 'most sure and certain of the virtues' (*Virt.* 216), the 'queen of virtues' (*Abr.* 270). To attain to it is no small matter; it is a 'task for a great and celestial understanding' (*Rer. Div. Her.* 93), it is the prize, which Abraham struggled to acquire.[3] It is associated as closely as possible with the virtue of piety,[4] it is the 'blameless and fairest sacrifice' to God

[1] Philo also uses *πίστις* absolutely in *Poster. C.* 13, *Conf. Ling.* 31, *Migr. Abr.* 43 f., *Mut. Nom.* 182 etc.

[2] *Leg. All.* II.89.

[3] *Migr. Abr.* 44, *Praem. Poen.* 27.

[4] *Migr. Abr.* 132.

(*Cher.* 85); and thus it is at the same time 'the only truth and certain good'.

Πίστις is therefore basically the firmness of a man, that which cannot be shaken, which by abandoning self is founded on that which alone is firm, alone has real being. In so far as this means turning away from the transient and turning towards the eternal, Philo is following the Platonic tradition, but in so far as he denotes this conduct as *πίστις* he is following late Stoicism. He seems to be deviating from it when he introduces into its concept of *πίστις*, meaning *loyalty to oneself*, imperturbability, the OT and Jewish meaning of faith in the sense of *trust*. This was of course easily possible, for faith and loyalty have an inner unity in the OT and Judaism. In place of the ἐφ' ἡμῖν which according to Stoicism should determine man's purpose, Philo has put God who is considered all through to be the object of faith. But since man's relationship with the fellowship of his nation and with history has been severed and God is not seen in his historical activity, so faith is directed towards pure being, which however can only be described in the main negatively as the Other. *Πίστις* is the attitude of withdrawal from the world in a purely negative sense; no positive apprehension of the Other can be arrived at by *πίστις*, but only by ecstasy. Man does not stand in *πίστις* before God in order to receive from him. But it is the goal of piety towards which a man trains himself by his own strength.[1] Indeed, *πίστις* is not a relationship of man with God, but, as in Stoicism, it is a relationship of man with himself.

[1] cf. Schlatter, *Glaube*, p. 61: 'Thus here too the believer turns to look back on his behaviour as a believer and makes this the basis on which his participation with God is to rest.'

ADDITIONAL NOTE

LXX rendering of 'mn etc.

He'^{e}mīn is rendered in the LXX 45 times by *πιστεύειν*; also 5 times by *ἐμπιστεύειν*, once each by *καταπιστεύειν* and *πεισθῆναι* (cf. TWNT, VI, pp. 3 f.), and in variant readings *θέλειν*. So too *πιστεύειν*, when it occurs, stands almost invariably for *he'^{e}mīn*, once each for the *niph'al* and *'aph'el* (in Aramaic) of *'mn*, once for *šm'* (= to *hear*; this is in Jer. xxv.8, but clearly for the sake of variety; in v. 7 *šm'* is rendered by *ἀκούειν*).

The other formations from the stem *πιστ-* are used almost without exception for formations from the stem *'mn*. *Πιστός* nearly always (29 times) represents the *niph'al* of *'mn*, and *πίστις* stands 6 times for *'^{e}met*, 20 times for *'^{e}mūnā*, but conversely *ἀλήθεια* stands 87 times for *'^{e}met* and 22 times, especially in the Psalms, for *'^{e}mūnā*. Besides, *'^{e}met* is reproduced 12 times by *ἀληθίνος*, and is rendered 6 times by *δικαιοσύνη* and 4 times by *δίκαιος*. It should be noted that *πιστεύειν* is never used for *bṭḥ* (cf. p. 26, n. 1).

It is noteworthy that *πιστεύειν* and *πεποιθέναι* never represent the same Hebrew original. On the one hand the *niph'al* and *hiph'il* of *'mn* are translated by *πιστεύειν* with philological exactness. The derivatives of this root in some cases have or receive in the LXX a quite different meaning, but are in general likewise translated by *πιστεύειν*, never by *πεποιθέναι*. Once only, in Prov. xxvi.25, *πεισθῆναι* is used in the sense of 'letting oneself be deceived'. On the other hand, *πέποιθα* certainly represents quite a number of Hebrew roots, even apart from *bṭḥ*, and these are reproduced in the LXX in very diverse ways. (In this respect *'mn* with its rendering in Greek by one word only is a direct exception.) But for none of the original Hebrew roots is *πιστεύειν* found as

a possible translation. This can hardly be accidental.

The LXX does not yet consider 'trust' and 'faith' as belonging together. *Πέποιθα* (=*bṭḥ*) is by this time a technical religious term. It is already used as such independently in the LXX, and is more frequent too in the later translators. On the other hand, *πιστεύειν* (=*'mn*) is scarcely yet felt to be a religious concept. The later translators have in this respect an attitude no different from that of the LXX. There is a change only in so far as amongst the Hexaplaric translators, Aquila and Symmachus especially prefer *πίστις* for *'emūnā*. Other special renderings of the LXX also disappear. But there are philological reasons for this. The Hexaplaric translators, however, also keep to *ἀλήθεια* for *'emet* (Bertram).

Πιστεύειν and its compounds are construed throughout the LXX with the dative of the person (similarly in Josephus [cf. Schlatter, *Jos.* 28] and in Philo), or with the dative of the object (e.g. *λόγῳ*, *ἀκοῇ* and the like, perhaps also *σημείοις* Exod. iv.9). Besides this, it is found construed with *ἐν* in I Kingdoms (I Sam.) xxvii. 12, Mic. vii.5, Ps. lxxvii.11, II Chron. xx.20 (Dan. vi. 24); with *ἐπί* and the dative in Isa. xxviii.16 (probably the correct text); with *ἐπί* and the accusative in Wisd. of Sol. xii.1; with *κατά* and the genitive in Job iv.18, xv.15, xxiv.22. Naturally *πιστεύειν* can also govern a *ὅτι* clause, e.g. Exod. iv.5, Job. iv.16, Lam. iv. 12, Philo, *Migr. Abr.* 18, *Rer. Div. Her.* 101; or an accusative and infinitive: Jos. *Ap.* II.160. The noun *πίστις* is construed with the genitive: Jos. *Ap.* II.218; or with *πρός*: IV Macc. xv.24, xvi.22, Philo, *Rer. Div. Her.* 94, *Som.* I.68, *Abr.* 268, 270 f., 273, *Praem. Poen.* 27; or with *περί*: Jos. *Ap.* II.169.

IV. THE GROUP OF CONCEPTS ASSOCIATED WITH *ΠΙ΄ΣΤΙΣ* IN THE NEW TESTAMENT

A. *Formal questions*

1. As regards the purely formal use of *πιστεύω* in the NT and in the other early Christian writings, there is only little that is peculiar as compared with Greek linguistic usage. As in Greek (cf. p. 37) *πιστεύειν* means to *rely on*, to *trust*,[1] or to *give credence to*.[2] It is construed with the dative of the person[3] or of the thing[4] and also with the accusative of the thing.[5] The Greek *πιστεύειν περί* is met with once only (John ix.18).[6] Naturally the absolute use is found also.[7] A *ὅτι* clause[8] and also an infinitive or an accusative and infinitive[9]

[1] A word in John iv.50; God in Acts xxvii.25, Barn. xvi.7, Herm. v.IV.2.6, m.XII.6.2 etc.; *πνεύματι* in Herm. m.XI.17.21.

[2] A word or the one who speaks it in Mark xiii.21, John iv.21.

[3] John iv.21, Acts xxvii.25, Ign. Rm. viii.2, Herm. m.I.2 etc. So too in Rom. iv.17 where the genitive is only the result of attraction. This must be distinguished from *πιστεύειν* with the dative meaning to *believe in* (cf. p. 58, n. 7).

[4] John iv.50 (*λόγῳ*), Acts xxiv.14 (*τοῖς . . . γεγραμμένοις*), II Clem. xi.1 (*τῇ ἐπαγγελίᾳ*), Herm., m.II.2 (*τῇ καταλαλιᾷ*).

[5] John xi.26, I Cor. xiii.7, Pol. viii.2.

[6] In Pol. vi.1 *πιστεύειν κατά* to *believe* (*something*) *against* (*somebody*) is found.

[7] Mark xiii.21, Luke xxii.67; I Cor. xi.18. *Πιστεύειν*, used absolutely in the religious sense, must be distinguished from this (cf. p. 72).

[8] Luke i.45; Acts ix.26, xxvii.25; John vi.69; Barn. vii.2; Herm. v.III.8.4, IV.2.4 etc. In these cases there is sometimes the shade of meaning *to consider possible*; see J. Jeremias, 'Beobachtungen zu nt.lichen Stellen an Hand des neugefundenen Griech. Hen. Textes', ZNW, 38 (1939), p. 120.

[9] Acts (viii.37), xv.11; Ign. Rm. x.2; cf. also Ign. Sm. iii.1. On Rom. xiv.2 (cf. below, p. 90).

can depend on *πιστεύειν*. The passive construction (to *be believed*) occurs as well.[1] Under the influence of the Semitic usage (cf. pp. 55 f.), *πιστεύειν* can also be used with *ἐπί* and the accusative[2] or dative[3] and also with *ἐν*.[4] But in particular the frequent expression *πιστεύειν εἰς*[5] in the sense of to *believe on*, found neither in Greek nor in the LXX,[6] is peculiar to the NT. This expression can scarcely be regarded as a development of *πιστεύειν* with the dative = to *trust*. Conversely the latter is often used following the analogy of *πιστεύειν εἰς*, that is to say in the sense of 'to *believe in*'.[7] On the contrary the fact that *πιστεύειν εἰς* and *πιστεύειν ὅτι* are equivalent shows that the phrase *πιστεύειν εἰς* is derived from the meaning of *πιστεύειν*, to *consider credible*, *true*.[8] *Πιστεύειν εἰς Χριστὸν Ἰησοῦν* (Gal. ii.16), *εἰς αὐτόν* and *εἰς ἐμέ* (often in John), and similar expressions, mean simply *πιστεύειν ὅτι Ἰησοῦς ἀπέθανεν καὶ ἀνέστη* (I Thess. iv.14, cf. Rom. x.9) or *ὅτι Ἰησοῦς ἐστιν ὁ Χρίστός* (John xx.31) and the like. Especially in John *πιστεύειν*

[1] II Thess. i.10; I Tim. iii.16; Herm. m.III.3; Dg. xi.3, xii.8.

[2] Rom. iv.5, 24; Matt. xxvii.42; Acts ix.42, xi.17, xvi.31, xxii.19.

[3] I Tim. i.16. Cf. Rom. ix.33, I Pet. ii.6, following variant reading of Isa. xxviii.16.

[4] Mark i.15.

[5] cf. TWNT, II, p. 430. Moule, *Idiom Book*, p. 69, 80.

[6] Apart from Sir. xxxviii.31 where there is a mistranslation; cf. v. 31b and R. Smend, *Die Weisheit des Sir* (1906), p. 351; also Helbing, *Kasussyntax*, p. 201.

[7] Acts xvi.34 (*τῷ θεῷ*. D has *ἐπὶ τὸν θεόν*); xviii.8 (*τῷ κυρίῳ*. D has *εἰς τὸν κύριον*); Titus iii.8 (*θεῷ*).—In John also *πιστεύειν εἰς* and *πιστεύειν* with the dative alternate; but they do so in such a way that *πιστεύειν* with the dative has its original meaning: to *believe in someone* (with reference to what he says); thus v.38, 46 f., viii.45 f., x.37 f., xiv.11. The alternation (e.g. within the verses 29 f.) is not due to the change of meaning of *πιστεύειν* with the dative (this can only be assumed in John viii.31 and I John iii.23) but to the fact that for John *to believe the words of Jesus* is identical in substance with *to believe in Jesus* (cf. p. 73).

[8] The Jewish formula *he'ᵉmīn lᵉšēm* (A. Schlatter, *Der Evangelist Johannes* [²1948] on John i.12) can therefore hardly be a parallel.

εἰς and *πιστεύειν ὅτι* alternate constantly with the same meaning.[1] The same is proved by the passive phrase *ἐπιστεύθη* (sc. *Ἰησοῦς Χριστός* I Tim. iii.16) and the fact that *πίστις εἰς* is not the equivalent of *πίστις* with the dative, but of *πίστις* with the objective genitive (cf. below, p. 60). Thus *πιστεύειν εἰς* is to be understood as an abbreviation which became a formula in missionary parlance,[2] an abbreviation which is all the easier to understand since the term *πίστις* played a part in heathen as well as in Hellenistic Jewish propaganda (cf. pp. 41 f., 48 f.). In so far as *πιστεύειν εἰς* (especially in the aorist) means to be *converted from* the Jewish or heathen to the Christian faith (cf. pp. 68 f.), *πιστεύειν εἰς* is to be understood on the analogy of *ἐπιστρέφειν ἐπί* or *πρός* with the accusative; this can be seen, for example in the juxtaposition of I Thess. i.8 (*ἡ πίστις ὑμῶν ἡ πρὸς τὸν θεόν*) and i.9 (*πῶς ἐπεστρέψατε πρὸς τὸν θεόν*). *Πιστεύειν* used absolutely often alternates with *πιστεύειν εἰς* and has the same meaning.[3]

Πιστεύειν signifying to *entrust* is also found not infrequently (Luke xvi.11, John ii.24); the passive is used in the same way.[4] This is not a specifically Christian usage, not even if Christ is the one who is the confidant (Ign. Phld. ix.1).

2. The noun *πίστις* has, as in Greek (cf. pp. 35 ff.) the

[1] cf. also Acts viii.37 (E) where *πιστεύειν*, used absolutely, which elsewhere alternates with *πιστεύειν εἰς*, stands parallel with the accusative and infinitive.

[2] Ign. Mg. x.3 is perfectly clear: *πιστεῦσαι* (=to *become a believer*) *εἰς Ἰουδαϊσμόν . . . εἰς Χριστιανισμόν*.

[3] On the other hand *πιστεύειν* used absolutely means to *believe* with the sense of to *trust*, to *have confidence* in Mark v.36, ix.23 f., xi.23 f.; this also occurs in Ps. cxv (cxvi).1 to which Paul alludes in II Cor. iv.13, whilst giving *ἐπίστευσα* a new meaning in accordance with the sense of the Christian term.

[4] Rom. iii.2, I Cor. ix.17, Gal. ii.7, I Thess. ii.4, I Tim. i.11, Titus i.3.

twofold meaning of *loyalty* and *trust*. Yet it is seldom used in the former sense.[1] It is found with the meaning of trust only in religious usage. Here it is mostly used absolutely, but can also be construed with εἰς,[2] with ἐπί and the accusative (Heb. vi.1), with πρός and the accusative (I Thess. i.8, Philem. 5). Nor has the construction with ἐν[3] a different meaning; and the objective genitive can also be employed instead of using prepositions to complete it.[4]

3. *Πιστός* too has both the Greek meanings (cf. pp. 34 f.) of *loyal* and *trusting*. It is often used in the profane sense of *faithful*[5]. So there is no question of a religious meaning for faithfulness when it is practised in the service of God (I Cor. iv.2, 17, vii.25); on the other hand it might be so used when describing loyalty to the faith (Rev. ii.10, xvii.14?) or when the μάρτυς (*witness*) is described as πιστός (Rev. ii.13).[6] But no religious usage is

[1] Of God's fidelity in Rom. iii.3; loyalty amongst fellowmen in Matt. xxiii.23, Gal. v.22, Titus ii.10; fidelity towards Christ in I Tim. v.12 (here πίστις almost means an oath; see Pr-Bauer); probably also in the traditional saying used in Luke xxii.32 (see Bultmann, *Die Geschichte der synoptischen Tradition* (³1957), p. 288), although the evangelist understands it as faith.—In Acts xvii.31 we find πίστιν παρέχειν in the Greek sense of to *give bail, submit evidence*; see M. Dibelius, *Aufsätze zur Apostelgeschichte* (1951), p. 54.

[2] Acts xx.21, xxiv.24, xxvi.8; Col. ii.5; I Pet. i.21(?).

[3] Gal. iii.26(?), Col. i.4, Eph. i.15, I Tim. iii.13, II Tim. iii.15; not Rom. iii.25 (cf. TWNT III.322).

[4] Mark xi.22; Acts iii.16, xix.20(D); Rom. iii.22, 26; Gal. ii.16, iii.22; Phil. i.27, iii.9; Col. ii.12; Eph. iii.12; II Thess. ii.13; Rev. xiv.12; I Clem. iii.4, xxvii.3; Ign. Eph. xvi.2, xx.1; Barn. vi.7; Herm. m.XI.9. There is no justification for the suggestion made by G. Schläger, 'Bemerkungen zu πίστις Ἰησοῦ Χριστοῦ', ZNW, 7 (1906), 356-8 to strike out the genitives Ἰησοῦ Χριστοῦ and Ἰησοῦ in Rom. iii.22, 26; Gal. ii.16, iii.22.

[5] Matt. xxiv.25, xxv.21, 23; Luke xvi.10 f.; I Tim. iii.11; II Tim. ii.2; cf. III John 5: πιστὸν ποιεῖν to *behave loyally*.

[6] Here Antipas is described as a 'faithful witness' who was not deflected from his witnessing even by death. It may be noted that

intended when the words of the Christian message are called *πιστός*, *trustworthy*, as in the formula *πιστὸς ὁ λόγος* (*καὶ πάσης ἀποδοχῆς ἄξιος*),[1] or when it is said of Christian prophecy: *οἱ λόγοι πιστοὶ καὶ ἀληθινοί εἰσιν* (Rev. xxi.5, xxii.6). There is just as little of a religious meaning when God himself or Christ is designated as *πιστός*.[2] *Πιστός*, *trusting*, is not employed in a profane, but only in a religious sense, and indeed with a Christian meaning and therefore denotes *believing*, *full of faith* (on this see pp. 81 f.).

4. *Πιστόω* is found in the NT only in the passive in I Tim. iii.16 meaning to *be made a believer*; similarly in I Clem. xlii.3. On the other hand in I Clem. xv.4 (from Ps. lxxvii [lxxviii].37) it has the meaning of *being faithful to*.

5. Amongst the privative formations *ἄπιστος* is found in Luke xii.46 perhaps denoting *unfaithful* (as contrasted with *faithful* in v. 42). Yet it is more probable that Luke intends the word to mean *unbelieving*, *not a Christian*.[3] It is often found with this sense (cf. p. 82). With the more general meaning of *unbelieving* it occurs in Mark ix.19 and parallels (*without trust*, *without confidence*) and in John xx.27 (with regard to the news of the resurrection, cf. v. 25). *Ἄπιστος* is used in Acts xxvi.8 to mean *incredible*.

6. *Ἀπιστέω* in Rom. iii.3, II Tim. ii.13 means to *be*

in Rev. i.5, iii.14, Jesus Christ is described as 'faithful witness'. Cf. TWNT, II, pp. 499 f.

[1] I Tim. i.15, iii.1, iv.9; II Tim. ii.11; Titus iii.8; cf. Titus i.9; see M. Dibelius, *Die Pastoralbriefe* ([3]1955) on I Tim. i.15. The formula is probably to be regarded as a fixed kerygmatic expression, cf. TWNT, II, p. 54.

[2] I Cor. x.13; II Cor. i.18; I Clem. xxvii.1, lx.1; II Clem. xi.6; Ign. Tr. xiii.3, etc. of God; II Tim. ii.13; Heb. ii.17, iii.2 of Christ.

[3] The passage comes from Q, the text of which may have been preserved in Matt. xxiv.51 with its *μετὰ τῶν ὑποκριτῶν* whilst Luke has altered it to *μετὰ τῶν ἀπίστων*.

faithless; in Luke xxiv.11, 41, Acts xxviii.24 (the opposite of *πείθεσθαι*) to *disbelieve* (words); thus also in the spurious ending of Mark in xvi.11; whilst it appears here in xvi.16 in the technical sense of *refusing to believe* the Christian gospel.

7. *'Απιστία* means *faithlessness* in Rom. iii.3 and Heb. iii.12. Heb. iii.19 (cf. *ἀπειθεῖν* in v. 18) shows how closely related to this is the meaning *disobedience*. For the general sense of *unbelief*, as lack of faith or trust see Mark vi.6 and parallels, ix.24, Matt. xvii.20 (variant reading); Rom. iv.20. For unbelief with regard to words see Mark xvi.14, to the Christian kerygma see Rom. xi.20, 23, I Tim. i.13.

8. *'Ολιγόπιστος* (cf. p. 48, n. 7) lacking in Greek and derived from Judaism, is found only in the synoptists: Matt. vi.30 and parallels, viii.26, xiv.31, xvi.8. The noun *ὀλιγοπιστία* is in Matt. xvii.20 (ℵB).

B. *The common Christian usage*

1. *The persistence of the Old Testament and Jewish tradition*

In primitive Christianity *πίστις* became the predominant designation of the relationship of man to God. This is due in part to the fact that, already in the OT and in Judaism, 'faith' had become a special expression for the religious attitude (cf. pp. 11 f., 49 f), and moreover that early Christianity, like Judaism, was a missionary religion. Faith means turning towards the God disclosed by the preaching. Thus in the common Christian usage the heritage of the OT and of Judaism is to a large extent brought out in what is meant by *πίστις* (*πιστεύειν, πιστός*).

(*a*) *Πιστεύω* often means to put faith in the words of God. Therefore faith applies to the 'scriptures' (John ii.22); to what is written in the law and the prophets (Acts xxiv.14); to what the prophets said (Luke xxiv.25)

or simply to the prophets (Acts xxvi.27); to Moses or his writings (John v.46 f.); and similarly to what God is saying at present, for example by an angel (Luke i.20, 45, Acts xxvii.25). John the Baptist can also be described in this sense as the one who is to be 'believed' (Mark xi.31, Matt. xxi.32); and the Johannine gospel (and this gospel alone!) says similarly that Jesus and his word are believed or ought to be believed[1]; for he is indeed sent by God (v.38) and speaks the words of God (iii.34 *et passim*). In fact, for John this means nothing else than 'to believe in Jesus' (cf. p. 73 and p. 58, n. 7). But it is characteristic of John that these two coincide.[2]

(*b*) It is brought out particularly in Heb. xi that, just as in the OT, to *believe* the words is to *obey* them (cf. p. 47). Here the *πίστις* of the OT personages has in some cases the more or less avowed sense of obedience.[3] How obvious it is for *πιστεύειν* to include the meaning of to *obey* is evident from the fact that the acceptance of the Christian preaching is expressed by *πιστεύειν* as well as by *πείθεσθαι* and that unbelief can be denoted not only by *ἀπιστεῖν* but equally well by *ἀπειθεῖν*.[4] It was chiefly Paul who emphasised that the nature of faith is that of obedience. For him *πίστις* is also *ὑπακοή*, as can be seen by comparing Rom. i.8, I Thess. i.8 with Rom. xv.18, xvi.19, or II Cor. x.5 f. with x.15. Faith means to him *to give heed* (*ὑπακούειν*) *to the gospel* (Rom. x.16); to reject faith means not to submit to the righteousness offered to faith in the gospel

[1] John ii.22, v.46 f., viii.45 f. etc.

[2] The unbelieving attitude towards (crucial) words can be expressed by *ἀπιστεῖν* (Luke xxiv.11, 41, Acts xxviii.24 [the opposite of *πείθεσθαι*], Mark xvi.11), or by *ἀπιστία* (Mark xvi.14).

[3] e.g. Heb. xi.4-6, 8, also 27 f., 30 f., 33. Correspondingly *ἀπιστία* = *disobedience* in Heb. iii.19 (cf. *ἀπειθεῖν* v. 18).

[4] In Rom. ii.8 the antithetic formula stresses that the proper relationship to God is one of obedience (cf. also Gal. v.7). On the usage of *πείθεσθαι* and *ἀπειθεῖν* cf. TWNT, VI, pp. 4, 11.

(Rom. x.3). He can call the acceptance of the gospel in faith *obedience in acknowledging the gospel of Christ* (II Cor. ix.13). He joins them together in *ὑπακοὴ πίστεως* (Rom. i.5).[1] For the theological interpretation of faith in these passages see pp. 87 f.

(*c*) Further, the meaning of 'trust', which in the OT and Judaism (cf. p. 47) is linked with 'faith', is not lacking in the NT, and it is especially prominent where the OT and Jewish influence is strong. Trust in God is mentioned relatively seldom (cf. TWNT, VI, p. 6). But it is natural for the *πίστις* of the OT personages in Heb. xi to be *trust* just as much as *obedience*; the paraphrase in v. 11: (Sarah) *considered him faithful* (*πιστόν*) *who had promised*, agrees with this. In fact *πίστις* in v. 11 is on the one hand trust that God will carry out his promise (cf. p. 48)[2] and on the other trust in his power to work miracles, as in vv. 17-19 and vv. 29 f. It is in this sense that the synoptists speak of faith in Jesus' miraculous powers.[3] In the Christian mission, this is replaced by faith in the wonder-working name (*ὄνομα*) of Jesus (Acts iii.16)[4] or in the power of the apostles to effect miracles (Acts xiv.9). In general 'faith' in the synoptists denotes trust in the miraculous help of God,[5]

[1] The phrase *εἰς ὑπακοὴν πίστεως* in Rom. xvi.26 and the words *ὑπηκούσατε* etc. in Rom. vi.17 agree with Pauline usage; but it may be that neither passage is really Paul's (cf. R. Bultmann, 'Glossen in R.', ThLZ, 72 [1947], p. 202).

[2] Similarly in xi.7, 8 ff., 13, 17, etc.; also in II Clem. xi.1; Herm. s.I.7, m.XII.6.2; correspondingly faith in God's future reward Herm. s.II.5; cf. v.III.8.4, 6.5.

[3] *Πιστεύειν* in Mark v.36; Matt. viii.8, 13, ix.28; in Mark ii.5, v.34, x.52; Matt. viii.10 and parallels; ix.29, xv.28; like a formula in Luke xvii.19.

[4] iii.6 reveals how the healing takes place, and subsequently in v. 16 it is said that *his name has made him strong*. The name is associated with the power (cf. TWNT, V, p. 276, Allmen, VB, pp. 278 ff., J. Pederson, *Israel*, I-II (1926), pp. 245-59).

[5] Mark iv.40, ix.23 f.

indeed in one's own power to perform miracles,[1] (so also in Paul in I Cor. xii.9, xiii.2). That such *πίστις* is basically faith in prayer is already intimated in Mark xi.22 by the fact that it is described as *πίστις θεοῦ*[2] and this is made clear by the saying added in Mark xi.24 in which *πίστις* explicitly means faith in prayer. The confident faith in prayer which does not doubt is described elsewhere too as *πίστις*.[3] In Paul the meaning of *πίστις* as trust is in general less prominent (but cf. p. 60); yet it is present when Paul is speaking of Abraham's faith as trust in God's power to perform miracles (Rom. iv.17-20). It is probable that the phrase *that he might be the father* in Rom. iv.11 is not intended to be a consecutive clause but to indicate the content of Abraham's faith; in that case the *πίστις* is the trust that God's promise will be fulfilled; similarly also possibly the phrase *that he might become the father* in Rom. iv.18. In Rom. ix.33, x.11 too, where Paul, alluding to Isa. xxviii.16 speaks of *πιστεύειν ἐπ' αὐτῷ* (i.e. God), *πιστεύειν* is intended to mean trust.[4] *'Απιστία*

[1] Mark xi.22 f. and parallels; Matt. xvii.20, Luke xvii.6.

[2] The *ἔχετε πίστιν θεοῦ* is an introductory addition of Mark (see Bultmann, *Die Geschichte der synoptischen Tradition* ([3]1937), p. 95), which is not found in the Q variants in Matt. xvii.20, Luke xvii.6, and which Matt. xxi.21 also avoids in the parallel to Mark. *Πίστις θεοῦ* is found only here with this meaning (Rom. iii.3 God's faithfulness); this is in line not with the OT and Jewish usage, but with missionary terminology (*θεοῦ* is missing in some MSS); cf. Lohmeyer, *Mark* ad loc.

[3] Jas. i.6, v.15; Herm. m.IX.6-12, cf. v.IV.2.6.

[4] cf. the even more colourless phrases such as 'to serve . . . in the assurance born of a good faith' in I Clem. xxvi.1 as a description of piety; Herm. m.I.2: 'believe him therefore and fear him' cf. Dg. x.i. In I Clem. xxxv.2 'faith with assurance' is reckoned amongst the blessings of salvation; similarly it appears in Herm. m.VI.1.1-2.10 as a virtue beside fear and self-control. In what follows *πίστις* is described as faith in the righteous or in the angel of righteousness. In Herm. s.IX.15.2 f. *Πίστις* appears as the first

is used several times with a corresponding meaning. In Rom. iv.20 it denotes lack of faith in God's power to work miracles, in Mark vi.6, ix.24 in that of Jesus, in Matt. xvii.20 (so in D, the Latin versions and Sinaitic Syriac) in one's own. *Ἄπιστος* has the same meaning in Mark ix.19. *Ὀλιγόπιστος*, taken over from Judaism (cf. p. 48, n. 7), has a similar sense.[1] We find *ἀπιστία* linked with double-mindedness in II Clem. xix.2 meaning lack of faith, i.e. of trust in general.

(*d*) There is a very close connexion between trust in God and hope (cf. p. 48 and p. 26, n. 1). This is emphasised in Rom. iv.18 by the words *In hope he believed against hope* and is evident also in the description of *πίστις* in Heb. xi. After all faith in God's promise is itself hope at the same time; and this meaning predominates in Heb. xi.[2] It is just for this reason that the OT personages can be examples for Christians whose faith is indeed also directed towards the future promised by God. Both of them know that they are *strangers and exiles on the earth* (v. 13)—the more so because the future promised to the faithful of the OT is really the same as that promised to the Christian[3] and neither has yet experienced the fulfilment.[4] The paradox of such hopeful trust is as strongly emphasised in Heb. xi as in Rom. iv.19. It is directed towards what is invisible (v. 7) or rather towards the one who is invisible (v. 27). For the sake of this paradox Heb. xi has, it is true, also accepted the Hellenistic (and Philo's) idea: *πίστις* is directed towards the invisible because this is not only the

of the virtuous virgins corresponding to *Ἀπιστία* as the first of the vices.

[1] Matt. vi.30 and its parallel speaks of the feebleness of trust in God, whilst in Matt. viii.26, xiv.31, xvi.8 lack of trust in Jesus' power to work miracles may be meant. In Matt. xvii.20 ℵ and B read *ὀλιγοπιστία* to denote the disciples' weak faith with regard to their own power to work miracles. [2] cf. Käsemann, pp. 19-27.

[3] vv. 7, 10, 14-16, 26. [4] vv. 13, 39 f.

promised future, but also the heavenly reality which cannot be perceived by the senses, but can only be believed in faith: *By faith we understand that the world was created by the word of God so that what is seen was made out of things which do not appear* (v. 3). And the preceding definition in v. 1 sums up both aspects: *Now faith is the assurance* (ὑπόστασις, cf. p. 26, n. 1) *of things hoped for, the conviction of things not seen.*[1] If this construction is put on faith, then it follows on the one hand that Heb. xi, which in other respects is couched in terms of the language of the OT, can understand faith in accordance with missionary terminology also: *For whoever would draw near to God must believe that he is and that he rewards them who seek him* (v. 6; cf. vi.1). On the other hand it causes special emphasis to be placed on that aspect of faith which turns away from this world and looks toward the heavenly world (vv. 7, 15 f., 24-26; cf. xii.2[2]). The element of hope in faith is also preserved where, in the specifically Christian usage (cf. p. 69), πίστις means faith in Christ. This is done in such a way that hope is named beside faith, but expressly distinguished from it. The less the Christian πίστις εἰς . . . as such is hope, the more hope (ἐλπίς), especially in Paul, retains its own element of faithful trust derived from the OT (cf. p. 26, n. 1). Πίστις and ἐλπίς appear side by side (and linked with ἀγάπη) in I Thess. i.3, I Cor. xiii.13, or in other combinations.[3] The fundamental connexion is emphasised in I Pet. i.21 in the words *so that your faith and hope are in God* (cf. p. 26, n. 1).

(*e*) The OT meaning of *loyalty* (cf. pp. 46 f.) is still discernible in πίστις. This is evident in the conclusion drawn from the remembrance of the witnesses to faith

[1] Πίστις can acquire this shade of meaning in Paul's writings too: II Cor. v.7.

[2] Paul draws the same conclusion in II Cor. v.6 ff.

[3] Col. i.4 f., 23, Heb. vi.11 (variant reading); cf. Barn. iv.8.

in Heb. xii.1: *let us run with perseverance the race that is set before us*, corresponding to what leads up to ch. xi: *for you have need of perseverance* (x.36). Hope and perseverance naturally belong together (cf. p. 26, n. 1). In the same way πίστις and perseverance are associated in I Thess. i.4[1]; similarly πίστις and patience in Heb. vi.12; also ἀγάπη, πίστις, service and perseverance in Rev. ii.19. The πίστις of the leaders who are held up as examples for imitation in Heb. xiii.7, is also to be understood essentially as loyalty; similarly πίστις has the same meaning when it is said in II Tim. iv.7: *I have kept the faith*[2] or when in Rev. ii.13 the church in Pergamum is praised: *you hold fast my name and you did not deny my faith.* Conversely ἀπιστία in Heb. iii.12 and ἀπιστεῖν in II Tim. ii.13 mean the *unfaithfulness* of Christians. In Heb. xi.17 it is said that πίστις holds firm in temptation and in Jas. i.2 f. that it produces steadfastness. In I Peter also the meaning of πίστις as loyalty is brought out, for it is to stand firm when tested.[3] When Paul is thinking of the 'faith' of Israel, the element of loyalty comes into play for him too. Thus in Rom. iii.3 he speaks of ἀπιστεῖν and of the ἀπιστία = the *faithlessness* of Israel. But where he enjoins loyalty to faith, he urges *to stand firm in the faith* (I Cor. xvi.13),[4] that is to say, πίστις as such does not mean loyalty, rather it is the *faith* to which loyalty is due.

2. *The specifically Christian usage*

(*a*) The specifically Christian sense of πίστις must be distinguished from all these meanings. It is indicated most clearly by the formula πίστις εἰς (cf. pp. 58, 60). Here πίστις is understood as the acceptance of the

[1] Also in Rev. xiii.10 (cf. xiv.12).
[2] For τὴν πίστιν τηρεῖν = to *keep faith* see Pr.-Bauer[4] s.v.
[3] I Pet. i.7; cf. also i.5, 9, v.9.
[4] cf. *stand firm in the Lord* Phil. iv.1, I Thess. iii.8.

Christian kerygma and consequently of the saving faith which recognises and appropriates God's work of salvation brought about by Christ. Naturally πίστις here too implies the sense of *giving credence*; and the elements of obedience, trust, hope and loyalty can also be included in the meaning—in the same way as conversely, where one of these senses is the primary one, the reference to Christ can be comprised in it.[1] But the primary meaning in the specifically Christian usage is the acceptance of the kerygma of Christ.[2] This usage is accounted for by its being in the first place missionary terminology (cf. pp. 48 f., 59). At first, 'belief in Christ' is used with the same meaning as 'belief in God', namely with regard to those who do not yet know the only God and do not yet believe in Him, but must first 'believe' in Him, namely in the sense of recognising His existence in order that they may then be able to 'believe' in Him in the sense of the OT conception of faith. Heb. xi.6 employs πιστεύειν expressly in the former sense (cf. above, pp. 66 f.). In fact the early Christian missionaries preached belief in Christ at the same time as belief in the only God whom the heathen are to confess, having rejected 'idols'. Thus the conversion of the Thessalonians is described in I Thess. i.8 as their πίστις πρὸς τὸν θεόν; and this expression is explained in v. 9: *how you turned to God from*

[1] Perhaps the clearest example is in Rev. xiv.12 where to πίστις =*loyalty* there is attached the objective genitive Ἰησοῦ which denotes the real subject of the kerygma.

[2] Rom. x.14-17 describes in detail how πίστις is the acceptance of the kerygma.—The kerygma is the object of faith in I Cor. i.21, ii.4 f., xv.11, 14; Herm. s.VIII.3. 2; so is the *gospel* (εὐαγγέλιον) in I Cor. xv.2; Phil. i.27(?); Eph. i.13; Acts viii.12, xv.7; Mark i.15; cf. Dg. xi.6;—the *testimony* (μαρτύριον) in II Thess. i.10, I John v.10; cf. John i.7;—*obedience* (ἀκοή) in Rom. x.16, John xii.38; cf. Herm. s.IX.17.4;—λόγος in Acts iv.4, xiii.48; Eph. i.13; Barn. ix.3; cf. xi.11 and cf. Barn. xvi.9.

idols (cf. p. 59). According to Heb. vi.1, *πίστις ἐπὶ θεόν* belongs to the rudiments of Christianity beside *repentance from dead works*.[1] In the OT and in Judaism (quite apart from propaganda) 'belief' is demanded as the appropriate attitude towards the God who has made himself known long ago and whose existence is not doubted. On the other hand, the early Christian kerygma brings the message that there is one God and together with it the message concerning Jesus Christ, His son, and of what God has done through Him and will continue to do. The acceptance of this kerygma is called *πιστεύειν*. It is therefore clear that in the specifically Christian *πίστις*, the element of trustful hope becomes less prominent. The *πίστις εἰς* . . . looks first and foremost at what God has done, not at what he is going to do.[2]

(*b*) In Rom. x.9 (cf. p. 58) Paul indicates the content of the Christian faith in one sentence in which he is consciously expressing, not a conception peculiar to himself, but that which is taken for granted by every Christian preacher: *if you confess* (*ὁμολογεῖν*) *with your lips that Jesus is Lord and believe* (*πιστεύειν*) *in your heart that God raised him from the dead, you will be saved.* Since in the synonymous parallelism *ὁμολογεῖν* and *πιστεύειν* have the same meaning,[3] it is clear that the Christian faith consists in recognising Jesus as Lord and at the same time accepting ('believing to be true') the miracle of the resurrection. It is obvious, and it is confirmed by other statements, that these tenets form a unity in themselves, and that therefore the resurrection is not

[1] cf. the manner in which in Acts xvii.22-31 the theological and Christological preaching is combined. Cf. also Herm. m.I.1; cf. p. 49, n. 2.

[2] See J. Weiss, *Das Urchristentum* (1917), p. 323; Wissmann, pp. 71 f.; Mundle, pp. 73-114.

[3] Belief and confession are also closely linked by Paul in II Cor. iv.13 (cf. TWNT, V, p. 209).

merely a remarkable occurrence, but is the fact of salvation on the strength of which Jesus became Lord. Naturally because they have this close internal connexion with each other, now the one statement, now the other, can be made alone, or the saving event may be described in other terms, or in more detail; but it is always the whole which is meant. *So we preach and so you believed* says Paul in I Cor. xv.11 with reference to the gospel (v. 1), to which it appertains *as of first importance* (ἐν πρώτοις v. 3) that Christ died for our sins, was buried and was raised on the third day and declared Himself to be the risen one. According to Rom. iv.24 Christians believe in *him who raised from the dead Jesus our Lord* (similarly Col. ii.12); according to I Thess. iv.14 *we believe that Jesus died and rose again.*[1] If the picture outlined in Phil. ii.6-11 of Christ's humiliation and exaltation is not explicitly denoted as the object of πίστις, yet it is to be understood as such. *To confess that Jesus Christ is Lord*—in so far as it is carried out by those on earth—is nothing else than a confession of πίστις (cf. Rom. x.9). The kerygmatic parts of the speeches in the Acts[2] describe the contents of πίστις, even if it is not always stated in so many words (as in xiii.39). For kerygma and belief of course belong together (cf. p. 69, n. 2; cf. I Tim. iii.16). Moreover it makes no difference whether in the place of the title of Kyrios[3] other titles are used to denote the honour due to Jesus, naming Him as the object of πιστεύειν; as for example in John xx.31: *in order that you may believe that Jesus is the Christ, the son of God*[4] or whether in the ὅτι-clause the work of salvation is described by means of

[1] cf. I Pet. i.21; Pol. ii.1.

[2] Acts ii.22-24, iii.13-15, x.37-41, xiii.26-37.

[3] cf. *Lord* in this series, esp. pp. 97 ff.

[4] cf. also John xi.27, vi.69, further I John v.1, 5, Acts viii.37 (so E and other MSS).

other concepts, as for example *that I came from the Father* (John xvi.27, 30), *that thou didst send me* (John xi.42, xvii.8, 21) or by the still more specifically Johannine: *that I am in the Father and the Father in me* (John xiv.10 f.) or by the simple *that I am* (John viii.24, xiii.19).[1] The salvation wrought by God in Christ can be designated as the object of faith in more general terms as the *love which God has for us* (I John iv.16) or by its significance: *But if we have died with Christ, we believe that we shall also live with him* (Rom. vi.8).[2] An epitomising expression for this saving faith is the formula *πιστεύειν* (*πίστις*) *εἰς*. . . .[3] In the place of the construction with prepositions the objective genitive can be used with *πίστις*.[4] In this sense *πίστις* and *πιστεύειν* can also be used absolutely, and this is so frequent in the writings of Paul, in the 'Deutero'-Pauline literature, in the Acts, in

[1] In the succeeding period the motive behind the wording was often to contradict a false doctrine, as e.g. Ign. Sm. iii.1.

[2] 'Faith in a divine spirit' in Herm. m.XI.9 probably means the belief that the divine spirit exists, or rather that it is bestowed within the congregation.

[3] *Πιστεύειν εἰς*: *εἰς τὸν Ἰησοῦν* in Acts xix.4, John xii.11; *εἰς Χριστὸν Ἰησοῦν* in Gal. ii.16; cf. I Pet. i.8; *εἰς τὸν κύριον* in Acts xiv.23; Herm. m.IV.3.3; cf. Rom. x.14; *εἰς τὸν υἱόν* John iii.36; cf. John iii.16, 18; *εἰς τὸν υἱὸν τοῦ θεοῦ* in I John v.10; *εἰς τὸν υἱὸν τοῦ ἀνθρώπου* in John ix.35; *εἰς αὐτόν* in Acts x.43; John ii.11, iv.39, vii.31, viii.30, etc; *εἰς ἐμέ* in John vi.35, xiv.1, xvi.9, xvii.20; Matt. xviii.6; *εἰς τὸ φῶς* in John xii.36; *εἰς τὸ ὄνομα* in John i.12, ii.23 (*αὐτοῦ*); in John iii.18 (*τοῦ μονογενοῦς υἱοῦ τοῦ θεοῦ*); in I John v.13 (*τοῦ υἱοῦ τοῦ θεοῦ*); *εἰς ὃν ἀπέστειλεν ἐκεῖνος* in John vi.29. *Πίστις εἰς*: *εἰς τὸν κύριον ἡμῶν Ἰησοῦν* in Acts xx.21; *εἰς Χριστὸν Ἰησοῦν* in Acts xxiv.24; *εἰς Χριστόν* in Col. ii.5; *πρὸς τὸν κύριον Ἰησοῦν* in Philem. 5; *εἰς ἐμέ* in Acts xxvi.18.

[4] *Πίστις* with objective genitive: *Ἰησοῦ Χριστοῦ* in Rom. iii.22; Gal. ii.16, iii.22; *Ἰησοῦ* in Rom. iii.26; Rev. xiv.12; *Χριστοῦ* in Phil. iii.9; *τοῦ κυρίου ἡμῶν Ἰησοῦ Χριστοῦ* in James ii.1, cf. Eph. iii. 12; *τοῦ κυρίου* in Herm. v.IV.1.8; see VI.1.2, 3.6; *τοῦ υἱοῦ τοῦ θεοῦ* in Gal. ii.20; Herm. s.IX.16.5; *τοῦ ὀνόματος αὐτοῦ* in Acts iii.16; *μου* in Rev. ii.13.

John's writings and later, that examples are superfluous. Mark and Luke have also been influenced by the usage.[1]

(*c*) The question therefore arises whether this epitomising phrase *πίστις* (*πιστεύειν*) *εἰς* . . . which came into being for linguistic reasons in the first instance, can acquire at the same time a meaning of its own, i.e. whether it can be used to denote a personal relationship to Christ as well; thus—since of course *πιστεύειν εἰς Χριστὸν Ἰησοῦν* is the gateway to salvation—'faith in Christ' would have essentially the same significance as the relationship with God.

Now it is worth observing that the relationship with God is practically never denoted in the NT by *πιστεύειν εἰς*.[2] Conversely the usual form of words in the LXX describing the relationship with God, *πιστεύειν* with the dative and *πιστεύειν ἐπί* with the dative (cf. p. 58), are practically never applied to the relationship with Christ. *Πιστεύειν* with the dative, which in Rom. iv.3 (17), Gal. iii.6, Titus iii.8, Acts xvi.34 (D: *ἐπὶ τὸν θεόν*) describes the relationship with God,[3] is indeed found frequently in John to denote the relationship with Jesus, but here it does not mean to *believe* (in Jesus), but to *give credence to* Jesus or his words. It is true that for John this is actually identical with *πιστεύειν εἰς* (*αὐτόν*) but must not be confused with it linguistically

[1] *Πίστις* in Luke xviii.8; *πιστεύειν* in Mark ix.42, Luke viii.12 f.; similarly in the spurious ending in Mark xvi.16 f.

[2] There are only two possible cases: (*a*) I Pet. i.21 (cf. p. 67). If this meant: *so that your faith and your hope are directed towards God*, then the *εἰς* would be caused, not by *πίστις*, but by *ἐλπίς* (similarly in I Clem. xii.7) in accordance with the linguistic usage attested since the LXX (see II Cor. i.10, Acts xxiv.15, John v.45. Cf. p. 26, n. 1. (*b*) John xiv.1: *πιστεύετε ἐν τὸν θεὸν, καὶ εἰς ἐμὲ πιστεύετε*. A unique case; the wording is chosen to express the oneness of Jesus with God.

[3] In addition Acts xvi.15 (D): *πιστὸς τῷ θεῷ*. Also in John v.24; I John v.10 *πιστεύειν* with the dative; but here in the particular meaning of *giving credence* (to God).

(cf. pp. 58 f.). Apart from these cases *πιστεύειν* with the dative is found only seldom applied to Jesus, and only once in the NT is a personal relationship with Christ expressed by it: II Tim. i.12 *οἶδα γὰρ ᾧ πεπίστευκα*, where the sense of 'trusting' is combined with that of 'believing in'; similarly also in Ign. Tr. ix.2. On the other hand in Matt. xxvii.42 (D), Acts xviii.8 (cf. xvi. 15); I John iii.23, as this passage in particular shows clearly it must be understood on the analogy of *πιστεύειν εἰς* (cf. p. 59). *Πιστεύειν ἐπί* with the dative in Rom. ix. 33, x.11; I Pet. ii.6; I Clem. xxxiv.4, quoting Isa. xxviii.15, denotes the relationship with God and is used for the relationship with Jesus only in I Tim. i.16, where the addition of *εἰς ζωὴν αἰώνιον* shows that the sense of hopeful trust predominates.[1] On the other hand the formula *πιστεύειν ἐπί* with the accusative, still rare in the LXX, is found several times and shows that the relationship with God and with Christ is the same.[2] For there is no doubt that it is not an epitomising formula, but denotes a turning towards the person of the Lord, just as *πίστις ἐπὶ θεόν* (Heb. vi.1; cf. Acts xvi.34 (D)) and *πίστις πρὸς τὸν θεόν* (I Thess. i.8; cf. p. 60) denote turning to God from heathenism.[3] In the same way *τὴν πίστιν ἣν ἔχεις πρὸς τὸν Κύριον Ἰησοῦν* in Philem. 5 shows that *πιστεύειν* can be

[1] The occasional *πιστεύειν ἐν* in Mark i.15, John iii.15 (?), and also *πίστις ἐν* in Gal. iii.26(?), Col. i.4(?), Eph. i.15, I Tim. iii.13, II Tim. iii.15; I Clem. xxii.1 must no doubt be understood not as a return to the LXX phrase, but as a linguistic variation on *πιστεύειν (πίστις) εἰς*.

[2] Acts ix.42, xi.17, xvi.31, xxii.19; Matt. xxvii.42 (D: *αὐτῷ*; 𝔎: *ἐπ' αὐτῷ*).

[3] The case is different in Rom. iv.24 (altered in Col. ii.12, I Pet. i.21) where *to them who believe in* (*ἐπὶ* + acc.) *him who raised from the dead Jesus our Lord* is construed obviously on the analogy of *ἐλπίζειν ἐπί* and has the same meaning (cf. Barn. xi.8). Similarly Rom. iv.5 (cf. iv.18).

used to denote a personal relationship with Christ.

But the crucial point is this: faith in Christ, as being the acceptance of the kerygma about Him, does not merely affirm the existence of a hitherto unknown divine personage, a 'foreign divinity' (Acts xvii.18). For the figure of Jesus Christ cannot be separated from his 'myth', i.e. from the history of the events of his life, death and resurrection. But this history is salvation history, i.e. the man who by his 'faith' affirms the kerygma, acknowledges thereby that this history took place for him[1]; and since Jesus Christ became Lord by means of His history,[2] the acceptance of the kerygma includes the acknowledgement of Jesus Christ as Lord, and indeed this finds expression in the phrase *πίστις εἰς τὸν κύριον ἡμῶν Ἰησοῦν* and similar ones. In that case *πιστεύειν εἰς Χριστὸν Ἰησοῦν* means in actual fact a personal relationship with Christ, analogous to that with God and yet differing from it. If the OT relationship with God is called 'faith in God', then faith of this kind is already different from the *πίστις εἰς Χριστὸν Ἰησοῦν* owing to the fact that the OT faith—as being obedience and loyalty—is directed towards the God whose existence is already always taken for granted. But faith in Jesus Christ, in its original and proper sense, is not obedience to the Lord who has always been known. On the contrary it is by faith that the existence of this Lord is first perceived and acknowledged. Faith lays hold of the conviction that for the believer this Lord, Jesus Christ, exists. For this Lord first meets him only in the kerygma, and he believes on the strength

[1] What is said in the NT by *ὑπέρ* and *περί* and similarly constructed formulae, is expressed later in phrases such as *πιστεύειν εἰς τὸν θάνατον αὐτοῦ* in Ign. Tr. ii.1; *εἰς τὸ αἷμα Χριστοῦ* in Ign. Sm. vi.1; cf. Barn. vii.2 (Barn. xi.8, cf. p. 74, n. 3).

[2] Phil. ii.9-11, Acts ii.36 (cf. Acts v.31 where He is made 'saviour').

of the kerygma, and in the future he can always only believe on the strength of this message. This never becomes a mere instructive piece of information, which might be dispensed with once it had become known, but always remains the foundation of the faith. For God instituted the word of reconciliation together with the Christ event (II Cor. v.18 f.). Therefore faith in the kerygma and in the person mediated by it are inseparable, and faith always remains a 'bold venture' in the sense that it is based on the kerygma.

So now individual passages show that the phrase *πιστεύειν εἰς Χριστὸν Ἰησοῦν*, which was originally a set form of words, can really express a personal relationship. Firstly Rom. x.9 proves clearly that to believe in Jesus Christ means to acknowledge him as Lord; and when according to Rom. x.14 *πιστεύειν εἰς αὐτόν* leads men to call upon him, then this *πιστεύειν* brings about a personal relationship with him, because it results in baptism. That faith passes into fellowship with him is shown by Rom. vi.8, Gal. ii.20, and in a special manner by Phil. i.29: *For it has been granted to you that for the sake of Christ you should not only believe in him* (*τὸ εἰς αὐτὸν πιστεύειν*) *but also suffer for his sake*, or by I Pet. i.8: (at the revelation of Jesus Christ) *whom not having seen you love, in whom* (*εἰς ὅν*), *though now you see him not, yet believing* (*πιστεύοντες*), *you rejoice* . . . , or by Acts xiv.2: *they committed them to the Lord in whom they believed.* To these must be added those few cases in which the relationship with Christ is expressed by *πιστεύειν* with the dative in the sense of *trust* (cf. p. 74)[1] and by *πιστεύειν ἐπί* (cf. p. 74) or by *πίστις πρός* (Philem. 5).[2]

[1] In later writings cf. Ign. Phld. viii.1 (cf. Pol. vii.3); Dg. ix.6.

[2] It is possible that Philem. 5 is even speaking of a love directed towards the Lord Jesus. But it is probable that an inversion has taken place (Lohmeyer, *Philemon*, ad loc.), so that *πίστις* felt for Christ and love for the saints are meant.

(*d*) The saving faith, which is denoted by πίστις and πιστεύειν—it may be absolutely or with a qualification—can be regarded from the point of view either of its origin or of its continuing existence. When repentance and πίστις are preached (Acts xx.21, cf. Heb. vi.1), the hearers are urged to repent and to become believers. Πίστις is understood as the acceptance of the Christian message, e.g. in Rom. i.5, iii.25, x.17; I Cor. xv.14, 17, and probably also in I Thess. i.8 (*that you became believers*); Rom. i.8, xi.20 (*you stand fast only through faith*) and in all the passages where Paul is speaking of *being justified* or of the *justification* ἐκ πίστεως as in Rom. iii.28, v.1; Gal. iii.24; Phil. iii.9 and elsewhere. Naturally it is used in this way also in the period after Paul.[1] Corresponding to this, ἀπιστία is the rejection of the Christian kerygma (Rom. xi.20, 23).

In other passages πίστις means being a believer, ranked amongst the believers. This is especially clear when the 'lifetime of faith' is mentioned,[2] and also probably in I Cor. ii.5; II Cor. i.24, xiii.5; Gal. ii.20; I Thess. iii.2, 5 ff.; in addition to Paul in Eph. vi.16, I Tim. iii.13, Jas. ii.1, 5 and elsewhere.[3] But it is often uncertain whether it would not be better to understand it as confidence, for πίστις is frequently used to denote not so much the fact of being a believer, but rather the emotional state, the state of activity, of being a believer. This is the case when mention is made of *the measure of faith* (Rom. xii.3),[4] of the weakness of faith (Rom.

[1] Col. i.4; Eph. i.15; II Thess. iii.2; Acts xiii.8, xiv.27, xx.21, xxvi.18; Heb. iv.2; Herm. v.I.3.4.

[2] Did. xvi.2, Barn. iv.9; cf. Herm. v.III.5.4: 'they are young in the faith'.

[3] 'Απιστία is used in I Tim. i.13 in the sense corresponding to this; so also in Ign. Eph. viii.2, unless this is not to be considered as a still more hackneyed usage, so that πίστις and ἀπιστία mean simply Christianity and heathenism.

[4] Cf. v. 6, which speaks of the *proportion* (ἀναλογία) *of faith* with

xiv.1)[1] or of its strength,[2] of the increase of faith (II Cor. x.15),[3] of steadfastness in the faith,[4] its abundance[5] or its superabundance (II Cor. viii.7), of the practice of it (I Thess. i.3: *remembering your words of faith*, cf. Philem. 6) or of its unity,[6] and in all those passages in which πίστις and ἀγάπη[7] are linked.[8]

(*e*) In all these cases it is self-evident that πίστις is the *fides qua creditur* (of course as applied to its object). But as the usage developed it came also to mean the *fides quae creditur*. When Paul can call the message requiring faith (*fides qua creditur*) the ῥῆμα τῆς πίστεως (Rom. x.8) or when he denotes it as the ἀκοὴ πίστεως (*the preaching which requires faith* or . . . *which opens up the possibility of faith* in Gal. iii.2, 5), it is natural for him to summarise it as εὐαγγελίζεσθαι τὴν πίστιν (*to preach the faith*, Gal. i.23). In this way the message itself can also be called

reference to the gift of prophecy, a gift which is particularly dangerous and in need of examination (cf. I Cor. xii.10, xiv.29) because it can be practised without πίστις (cf. TWNT, I, pp. 350 f.)

[1] cf. Herm. s.IX.26.8, and conversely Herm. m.V.2.3.

[2] cf. Col. ii.7: βεβαιούμενοι τῇ πίστει; cf. also Herm. v.III.5.5, m.XII.6.1, v.III.12.3; I Clem. i.2; Acts xvi.5; Col. ii.5; Ign. Eph. x.2.

[3] Phil. i.25: εἰς τὴν ὑμῶν προκοπὴν καὶ χαρὰν τῆς πίστεως, cf. Pol. iii.2.

[4] Col. i.23; εἴ γε ἐπιμένετε τῇ πίστει, Acts xiv.22; Herm. s. VIII.9.1; Did. xvi.5; cf. Ign. Sm. i.1.

[5] Πλήρης πίστεως in Acts vi.5, xi.24; cf. Herm. m.V.2.1, XII.5.4; Ign. Sm. introduction.

[6] Eph. iv.13: *until we all attain to the unity of the faith* (εἰς τὴν ἑνότητα τῆς πίστεως) *and of the knowledge of the Son of God*; cf. Ign. Eph. xiii.1, xx.2; Herm. s.IX.17.4, similarly IX.18.4.

[7] II Thess. i.3; Eph. iii.17, vi.23; I Tim. i.14, ii.15, iv.12; Ign. Sm. introduction; Herm. s.IX.17.4; 18.4.

[8] In addition cf. perhaps Rom. i.12, xiv.22 f.; II Cor. iv.13. We can however scarcely understand ἐκ πίστεως εἰς πίστιν in Rom. i.17 as meaning: *from becoming believers to having confidence*. Cf. also the phrase *from glory to glory* in II Cor. iii.18, and on this TWNT, II, pp. 254 f.

πίστις. Besides, Paul can use *πίστις* in the sense of a standard or a principle, since it is the attitude which God requires of men and as such is the way of salvation offered by God, as when he contrasts *νόμος* and *πίστις* as being the two paths to salvation (Rom. iii.31, iv.14) and speaks of the 'coming' of *πίστις*[1] as of an independent entity (Gal. iii.23, 25). Consequently he can form the combination *νόμος πίστεως* (Rom. iii.23).[2] *Πίστις* is also understood as a principle in Rom. iv.16, Gal. iii.12, I Cor. xiii.13. Therefore Paul can already use *πίστις* quite simply in the sense of 'Christianity', which again can mean being a Christian (i.e. Christian behaviour) or the Christian message, teaching, principles. Thus for example when he speaks of *οἰκεῖοι τῆς πίστεως* = 'fellow-Christians' (lit. those belonging to the household of faith, Gal. vi.10) or of *πίστις* as the object of *εὐαγγελίζεσθαι* (to preach) as well as of *πορθεῖν* (to destroy, Gal. i.21) and perhaps also when he says: *if prophecy, according to the proportion of faith* (Rom. xii.6).

Apart from Paul's epistles, *πίστις* is found meaning the preaching of the faith in Acts vi.7: *were obedient to the faith*; and as a principle in Eph. iv.5: *one Lord, one faith, one baptism.*[3] *Πίστις* as the *fides quae creditur* is meant when the *mystery of the faith* is mentioned (I Tim. iii.9; iii.16 tells what this is). Hence *πίστις* and *good doctrine* can be linked together (I Tim. iv.6); to succumb to false doctrine is called *departing from the faith* (I Tim. iv.1) or to *make shipwreck* or to *miss the mark as regards the faith* (I Tim. i.19, vi.21).[4] The right doctrine handed down by the Church is also *πίστις* in Jude iii.20, II Pet. i.1. Set phrases containing the word *πίστις* meaning

[1] The *coming of faith* marks for Paul a vital stage in the experience of salvation, i.e. the coming of the time characterised by faith in place of the time characterised by law (Rom. vii.9), cf. TWNT, II, p. 672.

[2] cf. *Law* to be published in this series.

[3] cf. also I Clem. lviii.2; Ign. Sm. x. 2.

[4] cf. I Tim. i.6 and II Tim. ii.18.

Christianity take the place of the adjective 'Christian' which had not yet come into use: *in a common faith* (Titus i.4); *according to the faith of God's elect* (Titus i.1); *in the faith* (I Tim. i.2, 4, Titus iii.15) or *in faith and truth* (I Tim. ii.7); *in the faith of Jesus Christ* (Ign. Mg. i.1).

(*f*) The meaning of *πιστεύειν* has developed and become differentiated in a similar manner. Certainly in most cases *πιστεύειν* means to *accept the message*,[1] especially when it is used in the aorist,[2] but also in the perfect.[3] The same sense is given by the participles of the aorist[4] and of the perfect[5] and of course by the imperative,[6] and *πιστεύειν* often has this meaning in clauses introduced by *ἵνα*.[7] The present tense now and then also has the meaning of *laying hold of faith* (*wishing to believe*).[8] The occasional linking of *πιστεύειν* with *repent*[9] and with *be baptised*[10] proves that *πιστεύειν* can

[1] cf. the synonymity of to *receive the word* with *πιστεύειν* in I Thess. i.6; Acts viii.13 f., xvii.11 f.; Luke viii.3. Corresponding with this *ἀπιστεῖν* means to reject the kerygma in Mark xvi.16; Ign. Eph. xviii.1.

[2] Rom. x.14, 16, xiii.11; I Cor. iii.5, xv.2, 11; II Cor. iv.13; Gal. ii.16; Acts iv.16, viii.13, ix.42, xviii.8 etc.; John iv.39, 41, vii.31, 48, xvii.8 etc.; Herm. v.III.6.1, s.IX.22.3; II Clem. xv.3; Pol. viii.2; Barn. xvi.7 (aorist infinitive).

[3] Acts xiv.23; II Tim. i.12; John iii.18, vi.69, xi.27; I John iv.16, v.10.

[4] Eph. i.13; Acts xi.17, 21, xix.2; Heb. iv.3; John vii.39; Mark xvi.16; Herm. m.IV.3.3, s.VIII.3.2, IX.13.5; Ign. Phld. v.2; II Clem. ii.3.

[5] Titus iii.8; Acts xvi.34, xviii.27, xix.18, xxi.25; Herm. v.III. 6.4, 7.1.

[6] Mark i.15; Acts xvi.31; John x.37 f., xii.36, xiv.1, 11; Barn. iii.6 (future).

[7] John i.7, ix.36, xi.42, xvii.21, xix.35, xx.31; I John iii.23.

[8] John i.50, iii.12, iv.42, vi.64 (?), x.26, xiv.10, xvi.30 f. In a different sense in Rom. x.9; I Tim. i.16; Acts xv.7; John iii.12, v.44.

[9] Mark i.15; Kerygma Petri (ed. Klostermann in *Kleine Texte*, 3 [1933]), iii.15; Herm. s.IX.22.3.

[10] Acts viii.12, xvi.31-33, xviii.8 (cf. ii.41, xi.18; Heb. vi.1 f.); Mark xvi.16.

denote that action of laying hold of the belief which is the basis of Christianity.[1] More rarely *πιστεύειν* means to *be a believer*, to *hold the faith*; yet probably the present must frequently be understood in this sense.[2] The timeless present of a proposition such as Rom. x.10: *for with the heart man believes unto righteousness* is somewhat different; here *πιστεύειν* can mean both *accepting a belief* and *being a believer*. The frequent use of the present participle in Paul and John has the same meaning.[3] That the sense has become less precise is shown especially in the use of the participle. The present participle is, it is true, still in some passages a genuine participle (*those who are the believing ones in me*), particularly when a qualification is added (*εἰς* . . . , *ἐπί* . . .),[4] or when the words 'we (you), the believing ones' are used.[5] But in other passages the phrase *οἱπιστεύοντες* stands simply for the term 'the Christians[6]'; the aorist[7] and the perfect[8] participles can be used in the same way.

When this point is reached, the meaning of the participle of *πιστεύειν* is merged with that of *πιστός*. *Πιστός* too is sometimes qualified by an object, so that the

[1] cf. also 'those that should believe' I Clem. xlii.4; Herm. m. IV.3.3, s.IX.30.3.

[2] Rom. vi.8; I Thess. iv.14; Acts xv.11; Luke viii.13; John xvi.9; Ign. Mg. ix.1 (2); II Clem. xvii.3, xx.2.

[3] Rom. iv.24; I Cor. i.21; Gal. iii.22; John i.12, iii.18, 36, vi. 35, 47, vii.38, xi.25 etc.; I John v.5, 13 (variant reading). Also I Pet. ii.6 (quoting Isa. xxviii.16); Herm. s.VIII.3.3. Often with *πᾶς*: Rom. i.16, iii.22, x.4; John iii.15 f.; I John v.1; Acts x.43, xiii.39.

[4] Acts xxii.19, Matt. xviii.6, John i.12.

[5] Eph. i.19; I Pet. i.8, ii.7, i.21 (so ℵ C 𝔎). Probably also Acts v.14.

[6] Acts xix.18 (D), II Thess. i.10 (variant reading), Mark ix.42.

[7] Acts ii.44 (?), iv.32 (?); II Thess. i.10; Herm. s.IX.27.11 etc. There is a curious phrase in Ign. Mg. x.3: 'in Christianity wherein every tongue believed'.

[8] Acts xxi.20, 25.

word acquires the verbal force of 'believing'.[1] Although this is still retained in the phrase *do not be faithless* (ἄπιστος) *but believing* (πιστός) in John xx.27,[2] yet it has usually been lost. The adjective πιστός means *Christian*,[3] the noun *the Christian*.[4] Corresponding to this is the use of ἄπιστος (cf. p. 61), which still has the force of a verb in John xx.27, but is mainly used in the technical sense of *not Christian*.[5]

3. *The relationship of Christian 'faith' to that of the Old Testament*

The manner in which Christians in general understood their faith in the NT and in primitive Christianity may be summed up as follows. When 'faith' is mentioned, it sometimes has the traditional meaning as in the OT and Judaism (cf. pp. 62 ff.), sometimes a quite fresh meaning (cf. pp. 68 ff.), although these two aspects

[1] Acts xvi.15; τῷ κυρίῳ (D: θεῷ); I Pet. i.21 (variant reading: πιστεύοντες) εἰς θεόν. On the other hand in the case of πιστός (Col. i.2; Eph. i.1) the ἐν Χριστῷ (Ἰησοῦ) is not a statement of the object but means 'those who are in Christ (Jesus)'; πιστός is therefore here used absolutely.

[2] Perhaps also in I Tim. iv.3; but in Rev. xvii.14 πιστός probably means *loyal*. Πιστός seems to have the force of a verb in the list of Christian 'virtues' in I Clem. xlviii.5 and in the combination πιστοὶ καὶ ἀγαθά in Herm. s.VIII.7.4, 10.1 or in the phrase 'for though one be a man of faith' in Herm. m.VI.2.7 and in 'faithful and strong men' in Herm. m.IX.9.

[3] I Cor. vii.14 (variant reading), I Tim. vi.2, Titus i.6, Acts xvi.1, Ign. Rm. iii.2, Mg. v.2, Herm. s.VIII.9.1. Cf. πιστὸς ἐν κυρίῳ = *Christian* in Herm. m.IV.1. 4.

[4] II Cor. vi.15; I Tim. iv.10, 12, v.16; Acts x.45. Cf. Ign. Sm. i.2. For πιστός in inscriptions see E. Peterson, *Εἷς Θεός* (1926), pp. 32-34, 309. Cf. Tertullian, *De cultu feminarum*, II.4 and 5 (CSEL, 69, 78 f.): *fidelis = Christianus*.

[5] I Cor. vi.6, vii.12-15, x.27, xiv.22-24; II Cor. iv.4, vi.14 f.; I Tim. v.8; Titus i.15; Rev. xxi.8; Ign. Mg. v.2; II Clem. xvii.5; Mart. Pol. xvi.1; Dg. xi.2.—In Ign. Tr. x.1; Sm. ii.1, v.3 it appears particularly as the quality of the teachers of false doctrines.

need not exclude one another (cf. p. 69). Their relationship will be made clearer if we consider the relationship between the specifically Christian idea of faith and that of the OT in general. In so far as *πίστις* (*πιστεύειν*) in the NT stands for belief in God's word (cf. pp. 62 f.), there is no difference in comparison with the OT and Judaism (cf. pp. 48 f.); and the specifically Christian *πιστεύειν εἰς* . . . (cf. p. 58) also includes this belief, since it is of course always at the same time belief in the preaching which brings the word of God. But this word of God has acquired a different quality (cf. p. 70). It is not associated with God's activity in the sense that it claims loyalty by reason of this activity or that it promises activity by God in the future. It is bound up with what God does in the sense that this is first revealed in this word.

In the OT the godly man believes (in loyalty and obedience) in God by reason of what He does; he does not 'believe' the actions themselves because they are plain to see in the national history.[1] In the NT it is precisely that which God does which is to be 'believed'; for that part of it which is exposed to view is the life of Jesus who lived on earth in the form of a servant and ended His life on the cross. That the 'foolishness' of the cross is divine 'wisdom', that the crucified is also He who rose again, who is exalted, who is the Lord, that thus, what was done to Him is a divine act of salvation —all this is not plain to see, but is only made plain by the words of the preaching. Consequently it may even be said that what God did is His word, so that John—

[1] In Ps. lxxii.32 too where God's wonders are mentioned as the subject of *he'ᵉmīn*, it is not a question of belief 'in' God's deeds, but of loyalty towards God on account of his wonders. Cf. Exod. iv.8 f. which speaks of *he'ᵉmīn in the voice of the sign* and then, in abbreviated form, *in the signs*, on the strength of which the people are to put faith in Moses.

drawing this conclusion—can call Jesus the logos, the 'word'. For this reason to *believe in the word of God* becomes *πιστεύειν εἰς Χριστόν*.

This already conveys the fact that when the NT requires faith, it involves no return to the position of the prophets (and the Psalms) of the OT. Faith is not the trust in God's fidelity to the covenant which has proved itself reliable and will continue to be so. For God's activity in which *πίστις* puts its trust does not demonstrate its nature in the fate of the nation as a whole or in that of the individual, but in God's eschatological action—for this describes what He effected in Christ—which brings all history to an end.[1] In so far as *πίστις* in this sphere means trust (cf. p. 64), it is trust in God's power to work miracles, which can awaken life out of death, and which will awaken us too, as it awakened Christ.[2] In so far as it is hope (cf. p. 66), it looks forward to the completion of the work of salvation begun in Christ, which is brought to an end, not in the glorious conclusion of a national history, but in the fulness of the Church. In so far as hopeful trust in a more general sense can spring up on the basis of the Christian *πίστις*—trust in Christ as in God—it is the hopeful trust that in the situation created by Christ between the moments 'no longer' and 'not yet', the Lord, i.e. God, will not let him who trusts in Him be put to shame.[3]

[1] With regard to this it is significant to note which are the blessings of salvation apprehended in faith; they are the eschatological gifts: forgiveness of sins (Col. i.14; Eph. i.7; Luke xxiv.47; Acts ii.38, v.31, x.43, xiii.38, xxvi.18 etc.); righteousness (Rom. i.17, x.10; Phil. iii.9; Acts xiii.39; II Clem. xxxii.4 etc.); salvation in the eschatological sense (Rom. i.16, x.10; I Cor. i.21; II Tim. iii.15; Luke viii.12; Acts xv.11, xvi.31 etc.); life (or eternal life) (Rom. i.17; Gal. iii.11; John xx.31; Barn. i.6, xi.11 etc.); spirit (Gal. iii.14, v.5 etc.).

[2] Rom. vi.8, viii.11; I Cor. vi.14; II Cor. iv.14.

[3] Rom. ix.33, x.11; I Pet. ii.6.

It is the faith that if we have died with Christ, we shall also live with Him (Rom. vi.8), that God will preserve him who believes until 'that day' (II Tim. i.12), for eternal life (I Tim. i.16). It is the hopeful trust which expresses itself in the sentences beginning with: *πιστὸς* (*faithful*) *ὁ θεός*[1] or *ὁ κύριος* (II Thess. iii.3, II Tim. ii.13), all declaring that God, or the Lord, will keep safe him who believes (Phil. i.6, ii.13). In so far as faith itself is loyalty (cf. pp. 67 f.), it is not loyalty in view of the mercy shown by God in the national history, but confidence in the act of salvation in Christ, the only 'name' which can bring salvation (Acts iv.12). It is a matter of remaining loyal, of 'standing firm' in the faith[2] in all temptations, above all in persecution. The obedience of *πίστις* (cf. p. 63) is not obedience under God's commandments which require law and justice for the national life, but the 'obedience of faith' to the one way of salvation opened up in Christ. It is of course also a turning away from sin—since salvation includes the forgiveness of sin.[3]

In every case *πίστις* is seen to be the act in virtue of which man separates himself from the world and turns round completely towards God in response to God's eschatological deed in Christ. It is the act on which the new eschatological existence of the Christian is founded and it is the attitude which goes with it.[4] *Πίστις*, being the attitude which constitutes a man's existence, has complete control of his life. So the absolute use of *πίστις* and *πιστεύειν*, not known in the OT (except in Isa. vii.9?, xxviii.16) and beginning to

[1] I Cor. i.9, x.13; I Thess. v.24; Heb. x.23.

[2] I Cor. xvi.13; II Cor. xiii.5; cf. Gal. v.i; Col. iv.12; Eph. vi.11 ff.

[3] cf. the combination of *πίστις* and *μετάνοια* (repentance), cf. p. 80, n. 9).

[4] cf. the combination of *πιστεύειν* and *βαπτισθῆναι* (being baptised), cf. p. 80, n. 10).

be developed in Judaism (cf. p. 49), becomes prevalent. Not until this point does 'faith' become simply the designation of the religion, and the 'believers' or 'those who have faith' are the Christians. As this action and attitude of faith, which is decisive for man, is directed towards Christ, it might seem as if the Christian faith pushed the relationship with God into the background. However the belief of those who place their faith in Christ is directed precisely to what God did in Christ. And the mere fact that the NT does not use *πιστεύειν εἰς Χριστόν* as an alternative to *πιστεύειν εἰς τὸν θεόν* indicates that God and Christ do not stand before the believer as two separate objects of faith—either side by side or the one subordinate to the other. On the contrary, in Christ, God himself meets him; and God meets him only in Christ. In Christ dwells the whole fulness of the deity (Col. i.19, ii.9). To put it another way, Christ is God's eschatological deed, beside which there is no room for any other deed claiming or promoting faith. Whilst the godly man in the OT is expecting further activity by God because of what he has already experienced, the godly man of the NT is still expecting only that the salvation already wrought by God will disclose itself fully. Christ is God's last deed, including the future in its scope.[1]

C. *Πίστις and πιστεύω in Paul*[2]

1. *Paul and the common Christian concept of faith*

(*a*) The common Christian usage, as it has already been described, making use of references to Pauline passages too (cf. pp. 62-82), is fundamental for that of

[1] The consciousness of this is clearly expressed e.g. in Heb. i.1 f.

[2] For the literature on this chapter see pp. xii f. and further the wealth of literature on Paul. Cf. e.g. Michaelis 116-38; Lohmeyer 62-156; Mittring 146.

Paul. For Paul too, who placed the concept of πίστις in the centre of his theology, it is not a spiritual attitude of man, but in the first place the acceptance of the kerygma,[1] i.e. submission to the way of salvation determined by God and made accessible in Christ. Thus for Paul too πίστις is always faith in. . . .[2] Πίστις and ὁμολογία therefore belong together, as stated explicitly in Rom. x.9 (cf. p. 70). In the ὁμολογία, the believer turns himself away from himself and confesses Jesus Christ as his Lord, and this involves at the same time a confession that he owes all that he is and has to what God has done in Christ. So Paul gives no more of a description than do the other NT writers of 'the psychological process involved in the development of faith'.[3] Thus for example in Gal. iii.23-26 it is the story of salvation which is sketched, not (in the manner of Philo) the dawn of faith in the individual; faith is exhibited by Paul as a historical, not as a psychological possibility. According to Paul the salvation effected in history is made real for the individual not in religious experience, but in the baptism performed on him (Gal. iii.27-29) and πίστις appropriates it. Thus it does not stand at the end of the road to God, as in Philo (cf. p. 53), but at the beginning. Even if πίστις is the devout acceptance of what the kerygma preaches, yet it is not restricted to a *fides historica*, because by confessing God's deed it acknowledges that it is valid for each individual. Πίστις, in that it is ὁμολογία, is at the same time ὑπακοή

[1] Rom. x.17: cf. p. 69, n. 2.

[2] On πίστις with the objective genitive cf. p. 60; on the interpretation in Paul see A. Deismann, *Paulus* ([2]1925), 126 f.; O. Schmitz, *Die Christusgemeinschaft des Paulus im Lichte seines Genitivgebrauchs* (1924); A. Wikenhauser, *Die Christusmystik des heiligen Paulus* (1928), *passim*; cf. Wissmann, pp. 68-75; Mundle, pp. 75-94 on πιστεύειν with εἰς cf. p. 58; with clauses introduced by ὅτι cf. p. 58.

[3] Schlatter, *Glaube*, p. 260.

(cf. p. 63), that is to say the actual recognition of the saving way of grace ordained by God. For *ὑπακοή* is the acceptance of the divine grace, because this grace is offered to man in the paradoxical form of the cross of Christ; i.e. because the divine act of grace means the judgement brought about by the cross on man with his sins as well as with his striving for righteousness or wisdom. So faith is the obedient acceptance of the divine verdict on the understanding of himself which man has had up to that point.

Thus the knowledge imparted by the kerygma and appropriated by faith includes both the knowledge concerning God's deed in Christ and also a new understanding by man of himself. *Πίστις* is the peculiar manner in which the divine *χάρις* is understood, and that means at the same time to know oneself to be under *χάρις*. Paul speaks of the knowledge of the believer in a double sense: first the knowledge of salvation communicated by the kerygma[1] and then the new knowledge of himself which comes to the man who believes.[2] The element of trust is also included in this knowledge of oneself through God's saving act. It is true that in Paul *πίστις* has only rarely the immediate meaning of trust (cf. p. 64) since it is in the first place *ὁμολογία* and *ὑπακοή*. But the use of *πεποιθέναι* (cf. TWNT, VI, pp. 6 f.) shows that trust (like hope, cf. p. 66) is part of faith. This element is distinguished from *πίστις* by the concept of *παρρησία*.[3]

(*b*) If *πίστις* is both *ὁμολογία* and *ὑπακοή*, then it is intelligible that not only the act of becoming a believer, but also the state of being a believer can be denoted by

[1] Rom. vi.8 f., II Cor. iv.13 f., cf. Rom. x.14-17.

[2] Rom. v.3, xiv.14; II Cor. i.7, v.6; Phil. i.19.

[3] This is a boldness or frankness towards God (e.g. Eph. iii.12) and towards men (e.g. Eph. vi.19 f.), including the idea of boldness in the gospel. Cf. TWNT, V, p. 881.

πίστις (πιστεύειν). For this purpose Paul can form the phrases πίστιν ἔχειν (Rom. xiv.22, Philem. 5), εἶναι ἐν τῇ πίστει (II Cor. xiii.5), ἑστάναι ἐν τῇ πίστει (I Cor. xvi.13, II Cor. i.24). The meaning of this last phrase is made clear by the parallel statements ἑστάναι ἐν κυρίῳ (I Thess. iii.8), in χάρις (Rom. v.2),[1] in the εὐαγγέλιον (I Cor. xv.1), namely that to be a believer signifies to belong to the Lord and to the grace made accessible by Him and declared in the gospel.

At the same time the contexts in which εἶναι and ἑστάναι ἐν τῇ πίστει are found, show that to be a believer is not a static condition, but that it takes place amidst the vicissitudes of each man's life, that it is has constantly to hold its own against the danger of falling (πίπτειν, cf. TWNT, VI, pp. 164 ff.).[2] Thus πίστις has not done all that it is required of it when the kerygma has been accepted, as though it were merely the declaration made on admission to a new religion. It has to maintain itself continuously as the controlling attitude to life in the face of temptations. This is evident e.g. from Rom. xi.20: σὺ δέ τῇ πίστει ἕστηκας which does not mean: *you stand in the faith*, but *you have won your position through faith*—which in this context denotes through faith alone, not by your own deserts—a clear allusion to the fact that to be a Christian is to be constantly relating oneself to God's act of salvation. Therefore although this appears to contradict the interpretation of πίστις as a single decisive action in turning to God's grace, yet degrees and possibilities of πίστις for individuals are mentioned. There are *deficiencies in faith* (I Thess. iii.10); there is growth in faith (II Cor. x.15); there is fulness of faith[3]; there is weak-

[1] cf. Gal. v.4: τῆς χάριτος ἐξεπέσατε.
[2] I Cor. x.12, Rom. xiv.4, Gal. v.4.
[3] Paul uses for this the words πληροφορηθῆναι (Rom. iv.21, xiv.5) or πληροφορία (I Thess. 1.5). By these he means being fully con-

ness of faith (Rom. xiv.1). If to be *weak in faith* in Rom. xiv.1 f. means the same as being weak with regard to the conscience in I Cor. viii.7-12, it becomes evident that a Christian practises his faith by knowing what he has to do on each occasion. Hence the curious phrase *ὃς μὲν πιστεύει φαγεῖν πάντα* (Rom. xiv.2) and hence in particular the formulation of the principle: *πᾶν δὲ ὃ οὐκ ἐκ πίστεως ἁμαρτία ἐστίν* (Rom. xiv.23). Although all believers stand in one and the same *πίστις*, their decisions about what to do and what not to do may diverge, because their *πιστεύειν* has to be worked out in the conduct of each one. The principle is: *Let each be fully convinced in his own mind* (Rom. xiv.5); for the faith that each man has towards God is always expressed in his own life: *The faith that you have, keep between yourself and God* (Rom. xiv.22). Thinking must be guided *according to the measure of faith which God has apportioned to each* (Rom. xii.3). In this matter it is a question not only of degrees and stages of *πίστις*, but also of the variations brought about by the different gifts and circumstances of individuals, as the connexion between Rom. xii.6 (*having gifts differing according to the grace that was given to us*) and Rom. xii.3 (cf. above) shows. So Paul can speak of an *ἔργον πίστεως* (I Thess. i.3) and he indicates the whole sphere in which *πίστις* must work itself out in the life of each one by the words: *faith working through love* (*πίστις δι' ἀγάπης ἐνεργουμένη*, Gal. v.6).[1]

Even in statements such as these by Paul, the fundamental content of the Christian faith displays itself

vinced and having firm confidence, which are qualities inherent in faith.

[1] cf. the rest of the passages where *πίστις* is combined with *ἀγάπη* (I Cor. xiii.13; I Thess. i.3, iii.6, v.8; Philem. 5) and with *ὑπομονή* (I Thess. i.3). In the list of virtues in Gal. v.22 *πίστις* can hardly mean 'the Christian faith', but only loyalty of men to one another.

more and more fully and clearly. But Paul has displayed it to its fullest extent by contrasting it to the exclusion of all else with the *ἔργα νόμου*, and by his thorough development of its quality of *ὑπακοή*.

2. *The Pauline concept of faith contrasted with Judaism*

(*a*) Faith and works. The novelty and the completely different quality of the relationship to God, which is presented by regarding *πίστις* as the acceptance of God's saving act and as involving continual reference to it, is expressed by Paul when he consistently and firmly attaches the blessings of salvation exclusively to *πίστις*. Whilst these are termed—as in Judaism—*δικαιοσύνη*, there follows for Paul that which is a paradox in Judaism, namely that *δικαιοσύνη* is bestowed as a gift to *πίστις*, that it is therefore not awarded to man by virtue of his works.[1] Man can only stand before God by virtue of his *πίστις* and never by virtue of his works.[2] The whole epistle to the Galatians is an attack on the misunderstanding which is still possible that *πίστις* would have to be supplemented by the performing of some kind of works of the law. By this it becomes perfectly clear that *πίστις* is the complete surrender of a man to God, and indeed a surrender which a man cannot in any way decide to make of his own accord—for in that case he would remain in the domain of *ἔργα*—but which can only be a surrender to God's grace, and thus only a response to God's act (cf. p. 85). But it is at the same time equally clear that this surrender is a motion of the will, and in fact a basic decision of the will, by which a man hands himself over completely. It is an act in which the whole man is himself involved, whilst in the case of the *ἔργον* he always stands

[1] cf. *Righteousness* in this series, pp. 46 ff.

[2] Rom. iii.20-22, 25, 28, iv.2, 5 f., ix.30-32, x.4-6; Gal. ii.16, iii.6 ff.; Phil. iii.9 etc.

beside what he accomplishes. Paul expresses the active quality of *πίστις* on the one hand by understanding it as *ὑπακοή* (cf. pp. 87 f.), on the other quite unconsciously by never calling it inspired, as e.g. Augustine does.[1] The believer has the spirit bestowed upon him, but *πίστις* is not a gift of the spirit.[2] Faith is the behaviour of the man who is 'crucified with Christ', who no longer lives as himself, but as one in whom Christ lives (Gal. ii.19 f.). If the paradox that *πίστις*, being a motion of the will, is a negation of the will itself, is not understood, the antithesis *πίστις*—*ἔργα νόμου* is easily misunderstood, as though *πίστις* were after all again thought to be a good work, an achievement[3]. In that case Paul's rejection of works would be interpreted as applying only to the works of the Mosaic law, whilst 'a certain measure of independent human activity' is always assumed when faith is an act of obedience.[4] But in actual fact there is no assumption of a certain measure of independent activity in faith. It is an act in the highest sense, and at the same time the opposite of every 'work', every achievement, because the act of faith consists simply in the denying of all that a man does to establish his existence. Paul does not think of the rejection of *ἔργα* in any kind of restricted sense, but as a matter of principle, and this is shown by the fact

[1] cf. H. Jonas, *Augustin und das paulinische Freiheitsproblem* (1930), pp. 54-62.

[2] The case is somewhat different when *πίστις* is mentioned in the thanksgivings in the introductions to the epistles (Rom. i.8, I Thess. i.3, Philem. 5; so also in Col. i.4). For Paul can certainly consider it a gift (of God) that a community has come to believe in Christ (Phil. i.29). But when in I Cor. i.4-7 he names what the spirit has given to the community, it is characteristic that *πίστις* is lacking.

[3] cf. the discussion of this antithesis in TWNT, II, pp. 647 ff. Cf. also *Law* to be published in this series, and Allmen, VB, pp. 224 ff.

[4] Mundle, p. 101.

that beside the antithesis *πίστις—ἔργα* there stands the other one *χάρις—ἔργα* with the same meaning,[1] and that Paul quite consciously contrasts *χάρις* with working which can claim a reward, and frames the antithesis *κατὰ χάριν* (*as of grace*)—*κατὰ ὀφείλημα* (*as a due*, Rom. iv.4 f.). It is clear too that when Paul demands of a believer that he should fulfil the law in a new sense, namely in *ἀγάπη* (Rom. xiii.8-10, Gal. v.14), the *ἔργα νόμου* are not rejected in view of what they contain (i.e. as the law of Moses), but in view of the manner in which they are carried out. Finally Paul sets out perfectly clearly the motive for rejecting works: the road of the *ἔργα νόμου* is the wrong road to salvation because man wishes to use it as a basis for his boasting, his claim on God.[2] Since by destroying human boasting, both the Jewish righteousness of works as well as the pagan wisdom are equally affected, it becomes clear that when Paul rejects *ἔργα* he is rejecting a definite—and in fact *the* characteristic—human attitude, namely man's attitude of being self-confident before God, or of trying to become so. Therefore *πίστις* appears to be genuine *ὑπακοή*, which is the basic attitude demanded by God and made possible by God's act of grace in Christ, as contrasted not only with the specifically Jewish, but also with the specifically pagan attitude, that of the natural man in general, who imagines that he can hold his own before God by his own strength.

(*b*) It is clear that, if *πίστις* is an attitude like this, it is not something a man achieves as occasion offers and amongst other things, but that it is a fundamental attitude to life, determining his conduct in every detail (cf. p. 89). It has also been made clear that to become a believer and to be a believer belong inseparably together (cf. pp. 88 f.), since the surrender of human

[1] Rom. iv.16, vi.14, xi.5 f.; Gal. ii.21.

[2] Rom. iii.27, iv.1 f.; cf. on 'boasting' TWNT, III, pp. 648 ff.

security by the act of becoming a believer must be carried through by the continual subjugation of the natural man. And in so far as *πίστις*, being genuine *ὑπακοή*, is the surrender of the natural man, it is the eschatological attitude made possible by God's eschatological deed. It is the attitude of the 'new' man. This eschatological quality of *πίστις* is indicated by the fact that the phrase *ἐν πίστει* stands as a parallel beside the phrases *ἐν κυρίῳ* and *ἐν χάριτι* (cf. p. 89). Now it is just these phrases which designate the eschatological existence: he who is *ἐν Χριστῷ* is a new creature (II Cor. v.17); the period of *χάρις* has taken the place of that of *νόμος* (Rom. vi.14, etc); the 'coming' of *πίστις* is the eschatological time (Gal. iii.23 ff.).

3. *The Pauline concept of faith contrasted with Gnosticism*[1]

(*a*) Paul has not developed the meaning of faith as contrasted with Gnosticism as fully as he has the contrast with Judaism; yet his statements are sufficiently clear. As an eschatological attitude *πίστις* must not be misunderstood as though it were already itself eschatological fulfilment. It is not as in Philo a disposition of the soul, not the reward, the prize of the contest itself (cf. p. 53). Its meaning is rather that the man who is justified through faith (Phil. iii.9) is constantly striving for fulfilment, pressing on to the prize (Phil. iii.12-14). In *πίστις* it is not the finality of the eschatological existence, as in *γνῶσις* as understood by the Gnostics, which is conceived as real. *Πίστις* does not escape from the temporary nature of historical existence, but it embodies the eschatological existence in this life on earth.[2] For as on the one hand it is always referring back to what God has done in Christ (Rom. x.9), so on the other it directs

[1] cf. *Gnosis* in this series.

[2] H. Jonas, *Der Begriff der Gnosis* (Dissertation, 1930), pp. 43 f.

its gaze to the future, to what God will do (Rom. vi.8: *we believe that we shall also live with him*). This reference to the past and the future form one whole (I Thess. iv.14), just because God's action in the past is His eschatological action which determines and controls all the future. The knowledge about the new life imparted together with the faith is concerned with the future (II Cor. iv.13 f., Rom. vi.8 f.; cf. p. 88). Thus beside *πίστις* stands *ἔλπις* (cf. p. 66). And if *πίστις*, regarded as reliance on God's grace, will not be brought to an end even in the eschatological fulfilment, but will 'abide' (I Cor. xiii.13), yet this present life in *πίστις* is after all a temporary one in so far as sight is still lacking: *for we walk by faith, not by sight* (II Cor. v.7). Our salvation has become through *πίστις* not a possession at our disposal, but a sure hope (Rom. viii. 24 f. Gal. v.5, cf. p. 26, n. 1).

(*b*) This corresponds with the fact that *πίστις* is man's awareness that he is under divine grace (cf. p. 88). For this *χάρις* is not a divine *δύναμις* in the Gnostic sense which is poured into a man and transforms his nature, destroying his historical being. It is on the contrary understood strictly as the grace of the God who is the judge. It therefore always meets a man as the grace of forgiveness, in which is included the condemnation of sin and the subjection of a man to the demanding will of God, who desires that good should be done. Thus it never allows a man to escape from the concrete circumstances of his historical life. Therefore as *ἔλπις* belongs to *πίστις* so also, as part of its nature, does *φόβος*. This is indeed not the fear which lies hidden behind all the eagerness of the natural man to win his salvation through his own strength, for the believer has after all not received a *spirit of servitude again unto fear* but a *spirit of adoption* (Rom. viii.15). But he is not removed from God's imperative; and the *φόβος* befitting

him is nothing else than the knowledge that he does not stand on his own feet, the anxiety not to fall away from χάρις whether in thoughtlessness or in the pride of his presumed security. Hence the paradoxical reason *God is at work in you, both to will and to work*, given for the admonition: *with fear and trembling work out your own salvation* (Phil. ii.12 f.). Hence the admonition to the Gentile Christians: *They* (the Jews) *were broken off because of their unbelief, but you stand fast only in faith. Do not become proud, but fear* (Rom. xi.20). How this fear becomes one with the boldness and confidence of faith is shown in II Cor. v.11: the phrase *knowing therefore the fear of the Lord* corresponds to *having therefore such hope, we make use of all boldness* in iii.12 and to *such boldness we have* in iii.4. Φόβος denotes the knowledge of the believer that he is in the sight of God (*κατέναντι θεοῦ*, ii.17 or *ἐνώπιον τοῦ θεοῦ*, iv.2). Hence the admonitions to stand firm in the faith,[1] for the believer is exposed to temptation[2] and must constantly examine himself.[3]

(*c*) If *πίστις*, as the Christian state of existence, signifies in contrast to Judaism the 'no longer', in contrast to Gnosticism it denotes the 'not yet'. For Christian existence in *πίστις* is the paradoxical existence within the historical life on earth, an existence in the 'no longer' and the 'not yet' at the same time, as it is described most clearly in Phil. iii.12-14. 'No longer', for the decision of faith has cast aside the past of self-confidence and self-praise (Phil. iii.4-8). But as this decision takes place under God's grace and does not take a man out of his historical life on earth, it must be carried through by continually working it out afresh and the 'forgotten' past is ever present in the state of having been van-

[1] I Cor. xvi.13; cf. I Cor. x.12; Gal. v. i; Phil. i.27, iv.1.
[2] I Cor. vii.5, Gal. vi.1, I Thess. iii.5.
[3] I Cor. xi.28, II Cor. xiii.5, Gal. vi.3 f.

quished. To this extent remembrance (but not remorse) is a part of faith, which 'forgets', not by putting out of the mind, but by no longer allowing oneself to be caught. 'Not yet', to the extent that the surrender of the old existence is just the surrender of the self-security which supposes that it can control its own existence, i.e. to the extent that this surrender excludes the possibility of receiving in exchange a new possession at one's own disposal. What has happened is not the exchange of an old possession, formerly at one's own disposal, for a fresh one under one's own control from now onwards. On the contrary the change from the former to the present state means to renounce every desire to possess in utter devotion to the grace of God. 'Not yet': having regard to man of whom in his historical life on earth it cannot be said that he 'has apprehended'; but 'nevertheless already' in so far as for him it is true that he 'has been apprehended by Christ Jesus'.

D. *Πιστεύω in John*

1. *Πιστεύω as acceptance of the message*

With the exception of I John v.4 where *ἡ πίστις ἡμῶν* describes the power which overcomes the world (*κόσμος*),[1] the noun *πίστις* does not occur in the gospel or the epistles of John. On the other hand the verb *πιστεύειν* is found very often, and particularly in the common Christian sense of the acceptance of the Christian message concerning Jesus. The content of the message can be given in different ways by a *ὅτι*-clause (cf. p. 57); instead of this, shortened expressions with *πιστεύειν εἰς* appear in several variations (cf. p. 72, n. 3). *Πιστεύειν*

[1] cf. on this TWNT, III, pp. 867 ff. and esp. p. 895, mentioning in particular I John v.4 f.

used absolutely is frequently found with the same meaning.[1]

2. *Πιστεύω εἰς and πιστεύω with the dative*

It is peculiar to John that instead of *πιστεύειν εἰς*, *πιστεύειν* with the dative can also occur (cf. p. 58, n. 7), and in fact without the linguistic difference involving a difference of meaning; that is to say, for John 'to give credence to the preaching of Jesus' (who tells the truth, viii.40, 45), or to His word (ii.22), His words (v.47) and 'to believe in Jesus who is being preached', mean the same thing.[2] This corresponds to the fact that John has united the preacher with what is being preached, a union not yet achieved in the synoptic presentation. In doing so John certainly does not intend to 'correct' the presentation of the synoptists. On the contrary it might rather be said that he wishes to correct the kerygma. For he wants to demonstrate that in the kerygma He who is being preached is Himself encountered and speaks. What the kerygma preaches as something that has happened—God's action—itself possesses the nature of the word. Therefore John can designate Jesus himself as the 'Logos' (i.1) and thereby he gives complete expression to the idea that God's word and action are a unity. In the word God's action is encountered and God's action is His word (cf. pp. 83 f.). Ἀκούειν can be synonymous with *πιστεύειν*.[3] 'To be-

[1] Thus e.g. *πιστεύειν εἰς αὐτόν*, *πιστεύειν* used absolutely and *πιστεύειν εἰς τὸ ὄνομα* . . . alternate with each other in iii.18; cf. the alternation of *πιστεύειν εἰς* and *πιστεύειν* used absolutely in iv.39, 41, of *πιστεύειν* used absolutely and *πιστεύειν ὅτι* in xi.40, 42, xvi.30 f., of *πιστεύειν εἰς* and *πιστεύειν ὅτι* in xi.25-27.

[2] cf. the alternation of *πιστεύειν εἰς αὐτόν* and *πιστεύειν αὐτῷ* in viii.30 f. In the same way *receive him* (i.12, v.43) is found beside *receive the words* (xii.48, xvii.8).

[3] John v.25, vi.60, viii.43, 47, xviii.37.

lieve in Him' is equivalent to 'to come to Him',[1] 'to receive Him' (i.12, v.43), 'to love Him'.[2]

3. *Faith and Salvation*

Believing procures salvation, when this belief is directed to the word preached by Jesus and proclaiming Him and is thus directed to Jesus Himself. This fact is expressed in the continually repeated and varied sayings that the believer has (eternal) life,[3] that he has passed from death to life (v.24, cf. viii.24), that he is not condemned (iii.18) and so forth.[4] It goes without saying that the meaning is: this faith alone procures salvation. It is true that John has not brought this out like Paul by the antithesis *πίστις—ἔργα* (cf. pp. 91 ff.). For the 'Jews' whom Jesus is attacking in the Johannine gospel[5] are of a completely different type from the Jews (and Judaisers) against whom Paul speaks.[6] The motive for the Johannine sayings concerning *πίστις* is not, like that of the Pauline ones, the question of the way of salvation. John is fighting for the right conception of salvation itself. And for him the characteristic name for this is not, as for Paul, *δικαιοσύνη*, but simply *ζώη*.[7] Now if this is so, there appears to be agreement between the Christian preaching and the 'world' to which it is addressed, in so far as all the world desires 'life' as its salvation. But it is just the purpose of the Johannine preaching to show that this agreement is only apparent. What all the world calls 'life' is no life at all, but only the semblance of life. The world

[1] v.40, vi.35, 37, 44 f., 65, vii.37.
[2] viii.42, xiv.15, 21, 23 f., 28, xvi.27.
[3] iii.15 f., 36, vi.40, 47, xx.31; I John v.13.
[4] vi.35, xi.25 f., xii.36, 46; I John v.1, 5.
[5] cf. on this TWNT, III, pp. 378 ff.
[6] cf. TWNT, III, pp. 382 ff.
[7] A translation of the articles on *ζωή* and *θανατος* (*Life* and *Death*) is to appear shortly in this series.

has its being, not in error, but in lying (viii.44, 55), and because Jesus speaks the truth, it does not believe Him (viii.46). The world does not dispute the demand for faith, as do the Jews of Paul, but would be prepared at once to believe that Jesus is the Son of God, if only He would supply evidence of His authenticity,[1] if He whose language it does not understand (viii.43) would only express what He says in such a way that it understands it (x.24), that is to say, if He would accept its criteria concerning what is true. But what He says is for the world only a *παροιμία*, a *figure* (x.6, xvi.25, 29) and only becomes a plain saying[2] to him who believes (xvi.25, 29). He cannot say it in the way in which they understand it, for in that case it would be something different.

4. *Faith as renunciation of the world*

It becomes evident from all this that the world has no idea what salvation, 'life', really is. Hence the Jews search the scriptures, thinking that they will find life in them (v.39),[3] and do not wish to come to Jesus in order to have life. They would have to turn themselves from lying to the truth. They would have to sweep away all the standards and opinions by which they had lived up till then, to abandon all their former certainties. It is just this, the renunciation of the world, i.e. a man's renunciation of himself, which is the basic meaning of faith. It is a man's self-surrender, his turning to the invisible (xx.29), to that over which he has no control.

The antithesis makes this perfectly clear. Men cannot believe because they 'receive glory from one another' (v.44), because by mutually acknowledging each other's position they gain their security, they con-

[1] vi.30; cf. the demand for a proof of authenticity in ii.18.

[2] Expressed in x.24 by *παρρησία*.

[3] *Ἐρευνᾶτε* is indicative, not imperative.

solidate their 'world' and shut it off at the top against God, because they do not desire the glory of God. Thus ch. vi makes it clear that the crowds cannot believe in Jesus as the bread of life, because they demand the kind of bread which secures for them their physical earthly existence. Thus v.1-16, ix.1-34 illustrate the fact that the 'Jews' do not tolerate the disturbance of their mode of life safeguarded by legal correctness. Thus v.17 ff. and ch. xi require that a man should abandon the ideas of life and death which are familiar and authoritative for him, in order to be receptive to that life which Jesus gives and which appears where the world only sees death. It is demanded that the world should give up the conception of a 'Son of Man', a Saviour, who when he comes will remain for ever (xii.34), which naturally means that it should abandon the conception that a time of salvation brought about by God's action will be a permanent condition of affairs on earth.

That believing is a basic renunciation of the world is demonstrated by a series of statements which say that the act of believing itself is not an activity of this world, but a happening rooted in the beyond, an act or gift of God Himself.[1] It is necessary to be 'of God', 'of the truth', to be able to hear His voice (viii.47, xviii.37). It is necessary to belong to 'His own' to be able to believe (x.26). Understood as mere dogma, such sayings would simply state that only he can believe for whom it is determined—which would certainly be ill in keeping with the call sent out to all the world to make a decision for faith and with the reproach of evil intentions (cf. pp. 99 f.). In fact those sayings state that the process of believing must be understood not as a happening of this world, but only as a miracle, and thus they describe faith itself as the act of removal out of

[1] vi.37, 44, 65; cf. Bultmann, *Johannes* on vi.45.

this world. Jesus has chosen His own out of the world so that they are no longer *ἐκ τοῦ κόσμου* i.e. that they no longer belong to the world (xv.19, xvii.14, cf. *κόσμος* in TWNT, IV, pp. 895 f., Allmen, VB, pp. 470 f.).

Furthermore that this is the nature of faith is demonstrated by the fact that its object is set forth as something incredible to the intelligence of the world. There is agreement between Jesus and the world that 'faith' is concerned with God, in other words, with the divine world. But the scandal which causes the world to lose confidence in itself or to decide definitely for the darkness is the fact that the Son of God appears as a man: *the word became flesh* in i.14.[1] For neither is faith by any means a dualistic philosophy of life, which makes a man whose security has perhaps become precarious renounce the world in order to raise himself up to a world beyond by speculation or devout meditation and feelings. The 'removal out of this world', which takes place by believing is not an act which a man can perform freely for himself, and for the achievement of which the word of Jesus would only provide 'the occasion'. Such an act would include the assumption that the divine world was at a man's disposal for him to lay hold of; and this assumption would itself demolish what it is intended to prove. On the contrary the removal out of this world is thought of as fundamental, because God is thought of as one who acts in freedom. Removal out of the world only becomes a possibility for man through God's revelation. His revelation is the eschatological event which brings the

[1] It is typical that in John it is not Jesus' cross which is the real scandal, as it is in Paul, that is to say, not the fact that His righteousness is open to question, but the scandal is His human nature as such, that is to say, that His divine quality is not demonstrable. In John the cross appears rather as the end of His human nature, as His being glorified.

world to an end, since it signifies judgement for the world,[1] so that the verdict issues in life or death according to a man's faith. It is only now, since *the light came into the world* (iii.19) that the possibility of belief and unbelief exists in the decisive sense.[2] Thus only now through the coming of the revealer has removal out of the world become possible. But it is just the revelation which is the scandal; the invisible becomes visible to an extent such as by the world's standards it neither could nor should become. God's son came in the flesh,[3] a man whose parents and home are known (vi.42, vii.27, 41), who does not conform to what the messianic teaching, i.e. the world's conceptions of God's revelation, requires (vii.27, 41 f.), who breaks the law, declares himself equal with God (v.17-19). He will build a new temple in three days (ii.20), will be greater than Abraham (viii.58), His word is said to preserve from death. Who does He claim to be (viii.53)? He refuses to produce His authority or admits it only in a paradoxical sense (ii.19, viii.28). The fact is that only by faith can the truth of His word be discerned.[4] Nor do His *signs* provide unequivocal authorisation complying with the demand of the world. They are misunderstood (vi.26) and their chief effect is to cause a scandal and finally to bring Him to the cross.[5]

All this shows that the removal out of the world must not be understood as flight from the world, but as the reversal, the shattering, of the world's criteria and appraisals; that it would be a misconception to suppose that the believer must be taken out of the world (xvii.

[1] iii.16-21 (cf. on this Bultmann, *Johannes*, pp. 111 f.), v.21-27, ix.39, xii.31.

[2] cf. R. Bultmann, *Glauben und Verstehen*, I ([2]1954), pp. 134-52.

[3] i.14 and, obviously against Gnosticism, I John iv.2, II John 7.

[4] iii.33; cf. for this Bultmann, *Johannes*, ad loc.; also on v.31-37.

[5] cf. Bultmann, *Johannes*, pp. 152 f., 161 and on vi.30.

15). On the contrary his rejection of the world means that he has renounced evil (xvii.15). For 'world' is for John not a natural entity, not, as in Gnosticism, a region which encircles a man with the compulsion of fate and is alien to his being, but a historical entity which is formed by those who turn themselves away from the light, from God. Each one has himself a share in its importance and power through his own conduct.[1] For this world the revelation is a scandal, because it calls this world in question; it is the judgement of the world (iii.19, xii.31). And faith is the act of removal out of this world by overcoming the scandal, that is to say, by abandoning all reliance on one's own power. Expressed positively, it is the acceptance of the revelation encountered in the word.

5. *The relationship of the Johannine concept of faith to that of Paul*

The inner agreement with Paul is evident, in so far as for Paul too faith is the surrender of reliance on one's own power, of the righteousness attained by one's own strength, of boasting (cf. p. 93). Faith is for John as for Paul not a good work, nor is lack of faith an evil one. Faith and unbelief alike are indeed decisions and to that extent they are action in the true sense.[2] The agreement between John and Paul consists also in the fact that faith has the quality of obedience. This is clear because 'to keep the word' or 'the commandments' can be used as synonyms for *πιστεύειν*. These phrases, which mean obedience to command,[3] are used by John with a different meaning, partly for the obedient accep-

[1] cf. Bultmann, *Johannes*, pp. 33 f.

[2] cf. Bultmann, *Johannes*, pp. 112-15 and on vi.28 f.

[3] Thus I Sam. xv.11 (LXX); Ecclus. xxix.1; Jos. *Ant.* 8.120; Matt. xix.17; cf. I Cor. vii.19.

tance of the word,[1] partly for the loyalty of this obedience.[2]

6. *The anti-gnostic character of the Johannine concept of faith*

But it is just as evident that John's attack is not directed against the peculiarly Jewish aspiration for righteousness for oneself, but against the world in general, of which the Jews are only a particular case. They are not prevented from believing because they rely on the law of Moses and their works, but because they are *ἐκ τοῦ κόσμου*.[3] Thus the Jews serve as representatives of 'the world' in general, as is shown clearly e.g. by the transition in ch. iii from an attack on the Jews to an attack on the world.[4] In so far as John is alluding to a particular expression of worldliness, it is to Gnosticism, which is attempting to establish itself again within Christianity itself.

When *πιστεύειν* is grasped as an act of complete removal out of the world (cf. p. 101), it can be understood to be a withdrawal from the world in the wrong sense. Whilst negatively it means to renounce the world, yet it must at the same time be positively to lay hold of the world above. Actually it may be said, and it is said again and again, that faith has life (iii.15 f., etc.), that the believer has already passed from death to life (v.24; I John iii.14), that he will never die (xi.26). Therefore in believing, the eschaton has already been reached and thereby the whole future of the world in time has been outstripped. The eschaton has become the present.

This is a terminology such as is known in Gnosticism

[1] xv.20 and probably also viii.51 f., xvii.6.

[2] Thus xiv.23 f., xiv.15, 21 (cf. Rev. xii.17, xiv.12). Similarly xii.47. Of Jesus' obedience to His vocation, viii.55. For an extension of the meaning of these phrases cf. pp. 109 f.

[3] viii.23, xv.19, xvii.14, 16, xviii.36; cf. viii.44, 47.

[4] cf. Bultmann, *Johannes*, pp. 103 f.

also, and its manner of expressing its concepts has largely influenced John's language. But it would not only be wrong to interpret this terminology by its meaning in Gnosticism. Its special purpose is to make a distinction from Gnosticism, and the evangelist takes over the latter's questionings in order to place them under the light of Jesus' revelation. In fact, John's concept of faith has an anti-gnostic bias, to be seen in his explanation of the peculiar relationship of the 'already' to the 'not yet' of faith. The 'already' or the 'no longer' which is comprised in faith, is obvious in so far as faith is the complete renunciation of the world and has life 'already'. But the believer has life 'only' in faith; he does not have it as a possession, as a quality belonging to his nature. He does not—as he would in the Gnostic sense—partake of the divine nature. John does not know that final phenomenon of Gnosticism, ecstasy, in which what belongs to the other world (in a peculiar self-contradiction) is to be made into a reality in this world.[1] To behold the glory of the Son is granted only by seeing Him who became flesh (i.14), and emphasis is placed on the reality of the incarnation in contrast to Gnosticism (I John iv.2, II John 7). To see the glory directly is reserved for a future existence beyond this world (xvii.24). So long as the believers are in the world, they must not imagine themselves to be removed from life in this world (xv.15). On the contrary they are exposed to the continual attacks of the world, as was Jesus Himself during his life in the flesh (xv.18 ff.). Now this means that faith cannot dissociate itself from its connexion with the word. It possesses what it 'already' possesses, in fact 'only' as faith in the word—and just this is how faith is removal out of this world in the full sense. For

[1] cf. H. Jonas, op. cit. (p. 94, n. 2), p. 21; H. Jonas, *Gnosis und spätantiker Geist,* I (^{2}1954), pp. 199-203.

God's revelation is present in the world 'only' as the word which challenges the world. Therefore faith is temporary by nature, and this is obvious too from the fact that the revealer Himself can certainly be said to know, but not to believe (cf. p. 108).

7. *Believing and Knowing*[1]

The act of believing therefore does not transfer a man into a state of being removed out of the world, but it is the act of removal out of the world which must be accomplished constantly anew, so that the whole of life is dominated by it through and through. This is shown clearly by the admonitions to *continue*.[2] Believing must become a *continuing in his word* (viii.31); whether or not believers belong to Him and continue in Him, depends on His words continuing in them.[3] To those who continue is promised also the knowledge of the truth (viii.32); and indeed the changing aspects of πιστεύειν are elucidated by its relationship to γινώσκειν. John cannot contrast πιστεύειν with γινώσκειν in the same way as Paul contrasts πίστις with ἔργα νόμου (cf. pp. 91 ff.), for γινώσκειν is not a way of salvation analogous to ἔργα νόμου and hence in competition with πιστεύειν.[4] Its relationship to πιστεύειν is more complicated. There is no distinction between the objects of πιστεύειν and γινώσκειν. Both believing and knowing are concerned with the fact that the Father sent

[1] cf. *Gnosis* in this series, cf. esp. 49 f.

[2] John particularly stresses the immutable and indestructible nature of the Christian experience of divine immanence. God is in Christ (xiv.10); the believers are in Christ and Christ in the believers (xv.4-7 etc.); cf. TWNT, IV, p. 580. cf. Allmen, VB, pp. 102 f.

[3] xv.4-7. Fidelity in belief can also be called *keeping the word* or *the commandments*.

[4] No doubt John intentionally avoids the noun γνῶσις in the gospel as in the epistles.

Jesus[1]; that he who believes (xvi.27-30), like him who knows (vii.17), is aware that Jesus, or alternatively His teaching, comes from the Father. If knowing reaches the truth (viii.32), so equally does believing in Him (xiv.1) who indeed is the truth (xiv.6). That He is the Christ is accepted as the object of faith in xi.27 and xx.31; in vi.69 as that of *πιστεύειν* and *γινώσκειν* combined. Since *πιστεύειν* not infrequently denotes the act of first turning to Jesus,[2] it is natural in those passages in which both verbs are used together in the order *πιστεύειν—γινώσκειν*, to understand *πιστεύειν* just as that first turning, and *γινώσκειν* as the knowledge growing out of it to which faith moves on.[3] But the reverse order is also possible (xvi.30, xvii.8; I John iv.16), and in these cases *πιστεύειν* appears to be the attitude arising out of *γινώσκειν*. That both can be used shows that we may not distinguish *πιστεύειν* and *γινώσκειν* merely as the initial and final stages, not to mention the fact that we would have to differentiate between two types of Christians, the 'pistics' and the 'gnostics', as happens in Christian Gnosticism. On the contrary it becomes evident, in opposition to Gnosticism, that knowledge can never soar beyond faith and leave it behind. All knowledge that starts with faith continues in faith; but all faith should also become knowledge. As all knowledge must always be imbued with faith, so faith comes to be its true self by knowledge. Furthermore, if it is realised that the relationship of the Father to the Son is never spoken of as faith, but only as knowledge, it is clear that this association of faith and knowledge describes human faith which must develop into knowledge, yet without ever reaching a final state

[1] Believing: xi.42, xvii.8, 21; knowing: xvii.3.

[2] cf. p. 80 and cf. the admonitions to continue, p. 107.

[3] vi.69, viii.31 f.; cf. x.38. Thus *to continue in him* can pick up again *to know him* in v.4.

of pure gnosis. Only when human existence comes to an end as an earthly human one will the faith which knows or the knowledge which believes be replaced by sight which will then no longer be directed to the glory of the Son veiled in flesh, but will behold this glory directly (xvii.24).

8. *Faith and Love*

The believer cannot realise the possibility of his being removed out of the world whilst he is within the world, in such a way as to make it actual to himself as a condition. For he is in fact only in faith a man who overcomes the world (I John v.4). But it is possible for his removal out of the world to be demonstrated, namely by his conduct. This is generally called keeping the commandments or alternatively the word[1] given by Jesus.[2] These phrases can describe the obedience and the loyalty of faith (cf. p. 104), and equally the conduct resulting from faith (xv.10; I John ii.3 f., iii.22, v.2). The double meaning of the phrases indicates the inner unity of faith and action, just as in I John iii.23 f. the substance of God's commandment is stated as the twofold one of believing and loving. The unity of believing and acting accords with the substance of the commandments, in so far as the action which they require is nothing else than love (xiii.34, xv.12; I John ii.7 f., iv. 21).[3] For since faith knows Jesus as the revealer of the divine love (iii.16), to believe is itself to receive His love, and by this receiving of love, loving feelings spring up in the believer. The love for one another is founded on the love Jesus shows to His own.[4] To *love*

[1] The meaning is the same, as is shown in particular by the change in I John ii.3-5.

[2] i.e. His *new* commandment, which is love; cf. John xiii.34, cf. TWNT, II, p. 550.

[3] cf. *Love* in this series, esp. pp. 61 ff.

[4] xiii.34; the καθώς means 'by reason of that which' as frequently in John.

one another (xv.11-17) corresponds to remaining in Him, or in His love (xv.1-10). Similarly I John develops in all kinds of variations the theme that we are under an obligation to love our brother because we have received the love of God, given to us by the sending of His Son.[1] Such love possesses the nature of demonstration, for: *in this shall all men know that you are my disciples, if you have love for one another* (xiii.35).

[1] I John ii.5, 9-11, iii.10 f., 13-17, 23 f.; especially iv.7-21, v.1-3.

INDEX OF REFERENCES

OLD TESTAMENT

GENERAL INDEX